The

Beautiful

Enemy

The

Beautiful

Enemy

America's Narcissism Epidemic

Rahmana Finney

For my father Michael Finney who taught me to speak up, my Grandmother Joan Brann who took such good care of me, and my daughter Lali Naimah who has loved me to health. A special thanks to my good friend Wazir Kabir who really supported this endeavor, and to Janaka Bowman Lewis (www.vanillabowmancenter.com) who graciously gifted me her talents and kindness.

Table of Contents

FORWARD

One of the worst things about intense oppression, such as slavery, sex trafficking, fascism, or any kind of tyranny inflicted on groups of people, is that those inflicted people are united by misery, usually for generations, against an oppressor that they must constantly stand up to, prove themselves to, and protect themselves against. When you are constantly in a state of defense, it forces you to be extra protective because you and your loved ones are generally in some degree of danger or at least a set of very stressful circumstances.

You must hold your cards close to your chest. You must move with more stealth than is usual, and you must be very strong and resilient to keep your antennae up for abuse, manipulation, and aggression. This causes a great deal of mental, emotional, psychological, and physical stress. It makes it almost impossible to have healthy relationships when you are constantly under stress, and it conditions you into a mindset of functioning in a way that is optimum for enduring pain and trauma.

Some outcomes of this are that you will have to hide things about yourself, conform to an atmosphere that demands your subservience, and thus become somewhat removed from your feelings. Absolutely everyone wants to be free and when you cannot have freedom you will eventually succumb to the pressure of having to limit yourself. This pressure produces disease, violence, mental illness, and depression. It creates an ideal environment for unhealthy behavior and feelings, and it means that relationship abuse, or abuse amongst your loved ones, is absolutely inevitable. But because you are all united under a certain kind of suffering, and this requires that you really need and depend on each other, you will tend to endure a high degree of dysfunction from one another. You almost have no choice. You cannot be out in a world that may kill you before you get home, alone and with no protection.

This state of affairs has occurred in all cultures with polarized communities throughout history, like the Jews and the Nazis, the Chinese and the Japanese, or the Hutus and the Tutsi's—pretty much everywhere war or conflict has happened. This 'enduring dysfunction' behavior is particularly detrimental to the most oppressed communities because there is little in this dynamic that awards admitting your faults; you are after all trying to be even more effective than normal, and even hyper-functional so as to avoid the abuse that inevitably comes from oppressors. The constant harassment, exclusion, denial, and targeting is exhausting. Sometimes you are just trying to be invisible. This enduring of dysfunction then leads to a type of 'supporting' of certain pathological behaviors, like how an animal will chew off its own foot to escape a trap.

Having been raised exclusively in the Black community in the U.S., I have noticed that we do not traditionally seek help for or even acknowledge these pathological behaviors or the effects of suffering in our community, one of which is mental illness, and this is absolutely assured considering the 400+ years of systemic racism we have endured.

It is incredibly complicated to say the least, for Black women to protect their sons, and protect themselves from violent men, and have those two people look very much alike. The same is true for Black men who have Black daughters and wives when they have been abused by their Black mothers. It definitely presents a tremendous conundrum with issues of love and care. It can weaken your ability to operate functionally. And the thing is, and I can only speak personally for my community of people of color, any kind of admission of weakness is very frowned upon. Appearing strong has been absolutely vital. The value of strength is of course cross-cultural and has persisted through-out time, but it certainly gains value in groups of people that are suffering under tyranny. It is necessary for survival.

So, for many, many decades, we have had to survive in an unforgiving climate to who we are, which is based on skin color and hair texture, and thus cannot be hidden. We learned to stuff our feelings of rage and despair deep down inside, and ideally find outlets for them in our music and art, but as well, have unfortunately expressed them within our relationships.

This being the case, I believe Black people in America, Indigenous people, and many people of color, really need to begin to be more aware of the signs of mental illness and start to address it, because we have a lot of it, and it is nothing to be ashamed of. It is evidence that oppression is detrimental to humanity. We would have to have been robots to get through genocide, being stolen from our home, forced into 400 years of slavery and torture, and a following 147 years more of torture and abuse via Jim Crow and racism.

No feeling, loving human being can make it through these experiences without significant damage. I truly believe this makes our situation unique. We have some special needs to put it mildly. And this isn't to say that all the Black people who are here come from this; many African and Indigenous people have been traveling to and from the America's for centuries. But this legacy of oppression, genocide, and slavery is a big part of the history of Black and Native people in the U.S., and clearly, there are still many, many people in power here who prefer that reality even today. At least they believe they do … but they really, really believe it!

In looking at all the books written about narcissism, I found no authors who were Black. But I know so many Black folk who grew up with mental illness and narcissism, and we certainly have had to deal with many narcissists through-out the history of this country, because racism is an extreme form of narcissism.

What is more narcissistic than 'I am better than you because of skin color?' Really, any type of superiority complex whether based on gender, race, class, religion, or anything else is narcissistic. Ergo, we need more information on narcissism and mental illness in general. We do not always have the adequate healthcare to respond to it, police clearly don't have the training to respond to it (and often don't care because they are under-paid and over-worked), and the health-care system is pretty much doing the best it can with a very limited healing tradition to address the issues of mental health.

Basically, there are no cures, but lots of treatments. There is also a strong history of experimentation on living subjects in allopathic medicine, and those living subjects are generally either in dire need, or without the power to object—in other words, people of color. A good example is the Tuskegee Syphilis Experiment.

There are multiple reasons that people of color need to be more vigilant in addressing narcissism and mental illness. Because there is a lot of it. And many of the people who have it have a lot of power … but many of them are also in our families. And hey, we are clearly a powerful people! It is almost unbelievable to have come out of this situation having produced Michael Jackson, Billie Holiday, Duke Ellington, Michael Jordan, The Williams' sisters, and now a woman of color is Vice President of this country. We are very strong and resilient, but we have suffered tremendously, and in order to really prosper, we must heal. In order to heal, we must begin to admit that we need healing. We are protecting each other; I get it, but is it protection? Or is it self-harm? And could we be unknowingly nurturing self-destructive behavior? And making it even easier for our oppression to persist?

It is almost unfathomable that all those people let R. Kelly get away with what he was doing. Michael Jackson was clearly a person in a lot of pain. It is said that no condition that is hidden can be healed; it must be revealed. We must take better care of each other. We must take better care of ourselves. We have to tend to these wounds.

INTRODUCTION

My brain finally snapped one morning when I was 16. I tumbled out of my bed in a drunken-like sleepy haze, stumbling across the freezing floor tiles of the hallway into the even colder bathroom. I had been suffering from insomnia for years and was never able to get a full night's rest, so it always felt like I was in a dream. When I would have to wake up for school, it was like trying to swim through seaweed in the dark. I vaguely saw my mother in my peripheral vision as I lurched towards the bathroom, but my bladder was pulsing with fullness and all I could focus on was getting to the toilet—especially since I had wet the bed well into my early teens. As I lifted my nightgown and lowered my bare bum onto the cold toilet seat, there was a sudden flurry of fists and arms striking me in the face over and over again, but the pee had already begun to creep down my urethra, so all I could do was sit, pee, and try to use my arms to block the blows to my face. Through the web of strikes, I could see that my mother had an enraged look on her face and was screaming at me "How dare you! How DARE you!" I was barely conscious and had no idea what I had done, and the only thing that came out of my mouth was, "can I just pee?" This stopped her in mid-attack, and she just stared at me for a few seconds with her eyes blazing and her mouth open, and she spat out "You will SPEAK to your mother in the morning!" and then she tore out of the bathroom.

So apparently my crime was not saying good morning to her. The rest of the morning was a haze of getting dressed, piling into the car with my little sister, and wandering through the halls of my high school from class to class. The most poignant moment of that day was when my good friend asked me at lunch, "What happened to your face?" I had completely forgotten to consider the scratches on my face, but I was astounded at how quickly I blurted out the actual truth. I replied, "My mom attacked me this morning while I was peeing."

Awk-waaaard. My unsophisticated 16-year-old mind had not prepared a lie. After what seemed like an eternity of silence, he asked, "Why?" I said, "I didn't say good morning before I went to the bathroom." I had never actually told anyone before that moment what was happening to me at home; it was like I had run out of the energy that powered my silence. I guess 16 years was my limit. The look on my friend's face showed such clear horror, that something in me realized there was something very wrong in my life. By 16, most of the emotion I was feeling about what I was going through had just drained out of me. I could not handle so much intense pain at that age, and so I just became a robot, numb to the craziness that continued for many more years. But a voice deep inside of me began to say every day, "You have to get away!" and so that became my focus. To get away. My mother had already told me that if I didn't get a scholarship, I would not be attending college. I put all my energy into getting good grades, and I got that scholarship.

I think one of the most painful realizations I had that day in school at 16, was that it was one of the milder events that I had experienced with my mother, and my stepfather as well, over the years. I almost laughed to myself at the look of horror on my friend's face because I was thinking, "Sheesh, what would happen if I told him about the other stuff?"

Like, the fact that my stepfather had forced me to strip naked before beating me when I was 8? The time he put my mother out of our van in the middle of the night on Cascade Road and drove away? When my arm was broken (basically because of him) and he waited 3 hours to take me to the hospital when I was 11? My mother forcing me to watch her give herself a vaginal exam? How she would starve me all day? That look of horror on my friend's face was the first inkling I had that something was terribly wrong. It had all been par for the course for me.

You know, this concept that whatever happens to you in your home when you are a child is perfectly normal to you because you have nothing else to compare to, is so difficult for a lot of people to understand. It is not until you get away and into the outside world that you begin to understand that something was amiss. Unfortunately, you have already developed coping mechanisms that you have had for years that are going to inevitably cause you even more suffering once you start trying to function in the outside world because, well, you are dealing with everyone the way you learned to deal with the people/person in your home, and that will only work with other crazy-ass people.

Now there are enough dysfunctional people and circumstances in the world for this to be effective a great deal of the time. I was constantly bullied as a child, mainly from dark-skinned girls who had been Jedi-mind tricked like so many Black girls into thinking they were ugly, so they hated me for my light skin, green eyes, and 'good' hair. I swear I thought my middle name was 'white bitch.' But I was also bullied by my cousin when I would visit my family in California, so even my temporary escape away from my mother was stressful. And I gave all of my bullies exactly what I had been conditioned to give, which was my complete compliance and submission.

There was often a strong under-current of confusion and pain in many of my interactions with people because I had no idea that I was approaching all my interactions from a place of having absolutely no self-worth. That is sweet smelling coffee for predators! So, the reality is, when you are raised in an abusive environment, it is almost a guarantee that you will be a mark for other abusive people and situations, because you operate in harmony with what they want—which is your submission to their abuse. This is most definitely what happened in my life. It is a double tragedy, and it really fucking sucks.

When I was around 25, my grandmother sent me a book entitled *Narcissism: Denial of the True Self* (Lowen, 1985), and as soon as I started reading it, I realized that this was exactly what my mother was! It was a profound realization, and the ability to be able to have some understanding of what I had been through was almost over-whelming. Up until that point (and really even long after as well because it takes so much to really get it), I was mainly subconsciously aware that something was wrong with ME.

This my dear readers, is exactly what being raised by or having any type of significant relationship with a narcissist will do to you. You are always operating and behaving from a place that is defined by the belief that something is wrong with you, or you are at least convinced that other people *think* something is wrong with you. Now depending on what your nature is, you could either internalize everything and be riddled with pain, anxiety, and physical and psychological health problems, or you take your frustrations out on others, which is clearly common. OR, you may compensate for this deep feeling of inadequacy by creating a much grander version of yourself that you present to the world to trick everyone into thinking that you are GREAT, even though inside you don't feel great. This is the seed of narcissism.

In essence, you either heal, suffer from obvious low self-esteem and struggle through life, or you develop the illusion of high self-esteem, become a narcissist yourself, and the cycle continues with all those that you then abuse. It's an old adage—hurt people hurt people. Now though, I think there are a LOT of hurt people.

I believe that we are presently caught in an era of a vicious cycle of the disease of narcissism, which is Narcissistic Personality Disorder, or NPD. This personality disorder has been growing and multiplying for some time now, probably at least since World II in the U.S., and possibly even since the 1600's considering the fate of the people who originally inhabited America and the state of the Africans that were brought here as slaves. These are two situations that would certainly require a lot of narcissistic people to pull it off and keep it going. Is there anything worse than slavery? I mean, it's not one of those things you can just get over and move on from. It is devastating to generations of people. Unfortunately, slavery has proliferated through-out history in many different parts of the world to this day. The types of people needed to participate in this would certainly need to have a basic level of callousness at best, and an anti-social personality type at worst. Considering the horrific details of abduction and restraint, removal by ship across the sea, the constant rape of children, women, and men, the whipping, branding, chaining, maiming and experimentation, family separation, mental and emotional abuse, malnutrition, neglect, the psychological pathologies created by life-long servitude, and all the people this entire process involved, we are talking about a good number of cruel human beings.

I believe we now basically have an epidemic, much like the Black Plague of Europe or the on-going HIV crisis and now the corona virus, of NPD. Seriously, how many serial killers have there been? How many corrupt cops, lawyers, and judges are there? How terrible is the state of our jails? Communities? We are no longer safe anywhere because of insane people shooting up schools, churches, movie theaters, malls, and jobs, and now they are often children. The use of anti-depressants and anti-anxiety medicines is at an all-time high along with addiction and physical illness. After centuries of tyrannical monarchies, violent dictators, wealthy sociopaths, sexually deviant religious leaders, and powerful people with absolutely no conscious or moral compass, we are in a period of constant turbulence. We are experiencing massive amounts of violence around the world, disease, failing social systems, poverty, hunger, and ecological devastation to our precious planet.

This assertion I am making about an epidemic of narcissism is made more poignant to me by the fact that in my and many other's opinion who have been trained in identifying this disorder, we Americans in our 'free' world, the great U.S.A., elected a POTUS that is a bona-fide narcissist. But I have also begun to notice that every other person I am talking to, feels like they have at least one person with NPD in their immediate family. So, let's take a look at this disease called NPD. Let's see what it is, why it is, who it is, what it does to us, and what we can do about it.

Chapter 1

THE DEFINITION

"I believe that man's cheese has fallen off his cracker." - The Green Mile (1999)

Introduction

Many epidemics and diseases have come and gone over the centuries, thriving or diminishing in our constantly changing world. We have traversed through numerous plagues, viruses, wars, famine, conquests, colonization's, the rise and fall of civilizations, technological advancements that have caused severe pollution and environmental changes, and produced corrupt monarchies and governments, various harmful medical treatments, and lots of intoxicants! There has just been a plethora of social, biological, and environmental factors that either support or destroy certain pathogens and circumstances. Put simply, a lot of shit has gone down, and we are still trying to figure out how to relieve suffering. Well, some of us are … clearly some of us are putting no thought at all into how to relieve suffering and are in fact significantly contributing to suffering.

These are the folks we are going to talk about! If you are reading this, it means you probably have or have had at least one person in your life that seems to be the source of significant pain and suffering for you. We are going to identify exactly what the deal is with those people in your life who are (consciously and unconsciously) contributing to, creating, and exacerbating your suffering on a regular basis. Considering the astounding figures on addiction in the U.S. over the past several decades, and the recent opioid epidemic, people clearly want to stop their pain and suffering.

I submit that one of the reasons behind the opioid epidemic, is a narcissism epidemic. I think people are in a lot of physical and emotional pain, and that the reason for much of that pain, is that people are being treated very poorly. And this includes physical as well as mental illnesses since science is finally admitting that stress causes illness. Most of us are willing to try almost anything to stop pain, and many of us will even resort to trying things that hurt us even more than we are already hurting because they provide temporary relief from pain. Thus, the opioid epidemic.

We should be able to agree at least, that the first step in finding a cure for a disease is the ability to identify it by the symptoms. We all know that if we have a runny nose and a cough, we have a cold, but if it's accompanied by high fever and painful body aches, it is the flu. Of course now we are all on alert for difficulty with breathing! We know that if we cut ourselves and it gets all white and pus-filled, we have developed an infection. Modern and ancient medicine have both developed a library of symptoms by which an ailment can be identified. Many of these are well-known to the average person, particularly with regard to physical ailments. Unfortunately, this is not the case with mental illness. We are in-fact just recently entering an era where there isn't a huge stigma associated with mental illness, and where those who are suffering from mental illness are deemed worth protecting because of their vulnerable state.

The abominable state of mental institutions goes back many centuries. True accounts on the infamous Broadmoor Hospital in West London, and the notorious report from Nelly Bly in her book *10 days in a Madhouse* (1887), are landmark examples of the horrors that occurred in mental institutions. There are many, many horror films based on some of the heinous things that have occurred at mental institutions, like the wildly popular television show *American Horror Story: Asylum* (2012). I think that most people do not realize that many horror movies and shows are based on actual true events such as *Psycho* (1960), which is based on psychopathic murderer Ed Gein, and *Scream* (1996) which is based on Danny Rolling, otherwise known as the Gainesville Ripper[1]. Considering the level of cruelty endured by patients that was reported in expose's on Broadmoor[2], and from the Women's Lunatic Asylum that Nellie Bly infiltrated by pretending to be mentally ill[3], perhaps these mental institutions were headed by some of our first narcissists ...

Just who are these people I am referring to as narcissists? This is an especially poignant question in a time where this term is thrown around a lot to describe someone. For the most part, people have considered the term 'narcissist' to refer to someone who is obsessed with themselves, or at least very self-centered. It has been used loosely not as a medical condition, but as a personality trait. The term itself originates from the Greek mythology about a hunter named Narcissus who is so beautiful that he causes his own death in one version, and another's death in a different version. There are many different versions of his story; one about him falling in love with his own reflection in water because he did not know he was looking at himself, and eventually committing suicide because he could not possess the image of who he thought was someone else; another where a young man named Ameinias fell in love with him and committed suicide when his love wasn't reciprocated by Narcissus, which resulted in the Gods he had prayed to cursing Narcissus and causing him to commit suicide[4]. In every version, Narcissus and/or someone else dies, all because he and others are completely captivated by his beauty and fall in love, which is always unreciprocated. I would say that this is an appropriate metaphor for the devastating destruction that narcissists cause themselves and all who they are involved with! Those who love them feel as if they will never ever truly have that love returned.

So, there are two very important plot points of this mythology, which represents a kind of distortion or illusion and unfulfilled desires. The first is a very strong element of duality, especially one of loving and not having that love returned. This is a huge part of narcissism and people who have NPD. One of the first most important things to understand about narcissists is that what they appear to be, and who they really are, are often two utterly and completely different things, BUT THEY DON'T KNOW IT.

My mother had a glowing personality in public! She was loved by many, and I mean MANY. Her students adored her, her colleagues respected her tremendously, and her friends thought she was wonderful. I remember attempting for the very first time to tell someone how violent my mother was, and the person out-right said, "No way, your mother is so gentle!"

I have this theory that one of the reasons so many people identified with the movie *The Matrix* (1999), is this underlying feeling for so many of us that people and things are very often not what they seem—especially in this modern age with so many physical and psychological altering agents like Botox, cosmetics, implants, anti-depressants, and social media. Much of what people appear to be is often a total illusion, and narcissists are the masters of illusions and lies. In fact, one of the very first metaphors for probably what is one of the original narcissistic archetypes, the Devil, is "the father of lies[5]." This mythology of manipulative, dishonest beings exists in all cultures, and is probably among our first methods of defining particular personality types.

The technical definition of NPD according to the *Diagnostic and Statistical Manual* (DSM-5), which is the reference used by experts in the mental health field, is: "A pervasive pattern of grandiosity (in fantasy or behavior), need for admiration, and lack of empathy, beginning by early adulthood and present in a variety of contexts[6]." Ok, so in layman's terms, this translates into "people who constantly try to appear larger than life, need everyone to believe they are great, and eventually don't give a shit about anyone else, unless pretending they give a fuck actually gets them some notoriety." Well, I have taken a good deal of license with my interpretation of that definition and added on that last sentence! We will get back to that later when we talk about the different types of narcissism … but it does go on to say:

"as indicated by five (or more) of the following:

(1) has a grandiose sense of self-importance (e.g., exaggerates achievements and talents, expects to be recognized as superior without commensurate achievements)

(2) is preoccupied with fantasies of unlimited success, power, brilliance, beauty, or ideal love

(3) believes that he or she is "special" and unique and can only be understood by, or should associate with, other special or high-status people (or institutions)

(4) requires excessive admiration

(5) has a sense of entitlement, i.e., unreasonable expectations of especially favorable treatment or automatic compliance with his or her expectations

(6) is interpersonally exploitative, i.e., takes advantage of others to achieve his or her own ends

(7) lacks empathy; is unwilling to recognize or identify with the feelings and needs of others

(8) is often envious of others or believes that others are envious of him or her

(9) shows arrogant, haughty behaviors or attitudes[7]."

We will get back to the last sentence in my personal interpretation above of the technical definition of NPD in a moment, especially since pretending or 'acting' and narcissism are serious hanging buddies (I would say actors and entertainers are the first group of people to be publicly identified as narcissists in modern culture). For now, let's talk about what the traditional narcissists actually look like.

Overt

Two of the types of narcissists are overt and covert[8]. Since overt narcissists are much easier to identify, we will start there. Over narcissists are the powerful people! The people we admire, look up to, and consider special. They are often devastatingly attractive, amazingly talented, fierce, brilliant, strong, accomplished, rich and/or famous. They have charisma and charm. They command respect. They seem confident, sure of themselves, and in control. They have style, presence, and status. Sounds like a lot of people doesn't it? Maybe even sounds like a lot of stuff that we all want?

This personality type is particularly celebrated now with the advent of social media and the commonality of fame as an accessible accomplishment for anyone. Today people are no longer always rich and famous because of their skills and talents; people can actually be famous just from being born into wealth like Paris Hilton or the Kardashians. I know it's hard to fathom from the point of view of what we value as a culture, but even though people have generally always desired wealth, fame was not nearly as common a goal as it is now in our recent history. This is a new phenomenon that has accompanied the age of the internet. There is suddenly this huge pressure for everyone to be FABULOUS. Of course, this is not a new phenomenon; this particular character trait was really promoted by Hollywood and the entertainment industry because ultimately that's what entertainment is about—making people feel good. You can't make anyone else feel good if you don't feel good, so appearing as if you feel great became a tool for power as an entertainer and in the entertainment business. This is probably why so many entertainers have had addiction problems. They have all been trying to uphold the image of being fabulous all the damn time. Having been an entertainer since the age of 9 myself, I know how it feels. I traveled around Atlanta with a children's theater group performing in musicals and I definitely had to be fabulous. Who wants to watch a grump? Boring. Unless they are very funny like Louis Black!

Then what is the problem with all of the adjectives above to describe someone? Isn't it awesome to be talented and accomplished? To have so many positives in your life? Well, first of all, there are very few people in the world who don't have some insecurities and fears, and if they don't, this often means they have anti-social personalities. Lacking normal fear is actually one of the character traits of certain anti-social personalities. Frankly, it's very often not totally honest when someone appears to be so fabulous all the damn time, and many famous people like the hilarious and very animated Jim Carrey eventually admit to this 'act[9].'

If you think about it, considering all the horrible things that have happened and continue to happen in the world, if you are even half-way aware, it would be difficult not to feel some sadness or anger from time to time. So right off the bat, anyone who always appears to be GREAT is probably hiding their more challenging emotions. Now that in itself is not terrible—we all hide things. But what if there are some people who are not hiding their sorrow or pain out of modesty, but because they actually can't even feel it? Because they have lost their ability for empathy long ago?

It is scientifically proven that certain drugs can damage the part of the brain that controls empathy[10] and it has been shown that repeated abuse can do the same[11]. A great number of these mean-ass unsympathetic people are pretty easy to identify as they are total curmudgeons and a drag to be around. However, there are clearly people (Ted Bundy/Jim Jones) who are very good at not only hiding the darkness inside of them but also creating and presenting an image of someone who is high functioning. These are the overt narcissists. The reason their greatness is so convincing is that they actually consciously believe this lie that they are great. Like they say, believe it and you will achieve it. The subconscious is another matter, but we will get to that …. anyhoo, the reason we often don't see the reality of who narcissists truly are, is because they can't see the reality of who they truly are. There was a collection of traumatic moments at some point when they were very young that eventually culminated in total dis-association to feeling pain. It was just too much for the young mind to handle a violent abusive parent, neglect, rape, or conditions of constant stress, and a subconscious mental process started so that they could alter themselves in a way that would create livable circumstances out of those conditions. A reality that is more palatable.

This is done to alleviate pain, create a tolerable situation, and achieve some level of balance and stability. Even the body is equipped with a biological mechanism to prevent us from feeling too much pain when injured; we refer to it as 'going into shock.' Well, the brain and heart are the same. For most of us, we need a psychological reality that creates an atmosphere that is more tenable for success, and everybody needs success. Success is the key component of the American dream—which in truth is just a condensed way of promoting the value of finding happiness and satisfaction with your life. Nothing wrong with that. Right now though, in our present circumstances almost more than ever, success means money. No money, no success. Money comes from getting people to pay you for something they want or need. You will have to develop and produce something that will provide this; a service, a product, or a skill that you can profit from. Unfortunately, this identification with being or doing something great can become a coping mechanism for someone whose self-worth has been seriously diminished. The term 'coping mechanism' is really just a fancy way to say, 'a way to survive.'

Now this is not an exaggeration! It is also scientifically proven that humans need more than just food, water and shelter to survive. We need connection, acceptance, and value. The babies in the crack ward of hospitals who are not held and cuddled have a higher mortality rate than those who are[12]. It is no small thing to say that narcissists are created out of a need to survive. It is the people who have been denied acknowledgement that will seek it obsessively because without it, we whither and shrink. We feel like nothing. And per our current culture of serial killers, psychopaths, sociopaths, and narcissists, this is obviously a dangerous thing.

So, who are overt narcissists, truly? Since the opposite of feeling like nothing is feeling awesome, understand that beneath that outer facade of grandiosity, greatness, and confidence is actually a person with a total lack of self-worth, and incredibly low self-esteem. It's just that it's all in the subconscious.

This is an often misunderstood aspect of narcissism. Narcissists were traditionally defined as having high self-esteem, but the truth is that the outer confidence is simply the 'Matrix' they have created to hide the real truth, which is that they actually have extremely low self-esteem. This is the part that really gets lost when people describe overt narcissists. The apparent high self-esteem is as I said, a facade. Think about it: If your wall is blue, why would you need to constantly paint it blue again? It is already blue. If you have good self-esteem, you do not need to be constantly reassured of your worth because you know it inherently. This is the reason narcissists go so out of their way to present this image of greatness—so that it can be acknowledged over and over. They need the applause. They need the award. They need the audience. They need it BAD. And they will do anything to get it. They will bully, coerce, lie, manipulate, steal, cheat, and use violence to achieve their goal. There is very little consideration for what they do and the effects it has on others; they are only focused on getting what they want and need.

That is the basic definition of the overt narcissist. These are people like the Roman Emperors Tiberius and Caligula, the head-chopping King Henry VIII, Adolph Hitler, Aleister Crowley, Idi Amin, L. Ron Hubbard, Donald J. Trump, Joan Crawford, O.J. Simpson, Jeffrey Epstein, and the 'Karen' types who rage through life destroying anything that gets in their way. Obviously this can lead to great success! Having very little care for other people's pain allows one a much wider field for achievement because nothing will deter you from your goal. They have no problem with causing other people's suffering. They will murder, rape, go to war, manipulate, and brazenly run rough-shod over anyone that gets in their way. In fact, like O.J. and many others on the list above, being able to just run over other human being is the one thing you most consistently need to do to acquire that fame and notoriety.

What we have unknowingly done is celebrated certain personality types. They are captivating, passionate, wildly charismatic, and unstoppable. They want to be the leader. Whether with a family, a team, or a country, they want to stand out in front. They want to walk on the red carpet, in the bright lights, out on the balcony, for all to see and all to hear. They create entire religions, countries, and legacies.

For the most part, overt narcissists have been male, but if you have watched any episodes of *Deadly Women* (2005), the slow leveling-out of gender roles in our culture has accommodated for women to be overt narcissists as well. Queen Victoria was ruler during Britain's' most expansive colonial rule around the world, which included slavery here in North America. For the most part so far however, or at least based on how the evidence has been interpreted, overt narcissists are mostly male. This has led to the creation of criminal profiles for sociopaths and psychopaths (who are always narcissists) as mainly violent and male. Many studies have been done on serial killers and this is what the research has shown.

Women have thus fallen into this "safe" category with the position of having been mainly victims of patriarchal domination, which is absolutely true to some extent, but definitely less than a full picture. Part of that male patriarchy is the idea that women are weaker, and thus are victims because they simply are not capable of the type of evil that men do, and this 'un-equalness' is one of the most dangerous aspects of sexism, or any ism for that matter. When you separate what people are capable of by particular groups that they belong to, you are creating circumstances that will nurture destructive behavior because you are automatically turning a blind eye to the reality of the multi-dimensional beings that we all are. One of these is the covert narcissist, and they can be just as destructive as the overt narcissists, possibly even more-so because they are under the radar. What is hidden is certainly more challenging to identify, and as stated, something that cannot be identified certainly cannot be cured. Nevertheless, so far covert narcissists are usually women, and the descriptive traits are a bit different.

Covert

Another reason it is important to recognize that narcissists actually have very low self-esteem is also the key to understanding covert narcissists. Because narcissists have been defined as having high self-esteem, we can easily overlook another category of narcissist, which is the covert narcissist. Covert narcissists are much more difficult to identify. They do not wield that grandiosity like overt narcissists do. They tend to seem to be self-effacing, a bit fragile, extremely sensitive, and they often present as a victim of other people's bad behavior. We are talking serial killers Karla Homolka and Aileen Wuornos, the women who have been diagnosed with Munchausen syndrome by proxy, which are the mothers who keep their children sick, even killing them eventually to get attention like in the movie *The 6th Sense* (1999), and the infamous Jim Jones. Jim Jones is one of the few notorious men I can think of who really defies the gender quality of this title, being the outwardly compassionate savior of homeless people of color that he seemed to be. Interestingly, upon looking deeper into Jim Jones, the reality is that he was actually physically and sexually abusing many of the members of his church before he moved it to Guyana[13].

Another great example of an anomaly with regard to the usual gender exclusivity of covert narcissism is film-maker Woody Allen. After watching the HBO documentary *Allen v. Farrow* (2021), it was very obvious to me that he had many of the classic characteristics of a covert narcissist. He has always presented as very self-effacing, insecure, weak, and depressed. He is probably the originator of the 'Beta male' star that got so popular in the last decade or two like Jonah Hill and Seth Rogen. Allen seems so absolutely unthreatening, but underneath the constant coughing, diminutive cast-down eyes and terrible posture when interviewed, he was a predator and a pedophile.

I found it fascinating to identify yet another category of prowess that causes people to deny the possibility of criminal behavior. In addition to the gifts of good looks, strength, or talent, intellectual capability is also a great distractor. Allen was consistently referred to as incredibly talented and creative, a philosopher, and a brilliant artist. This made it difficult to say the least, for those whose careers benefitted from his work, to believe his daughter when she consistently reported his sexual abuse of her.

Like the definition of the word covert, everything is much more hidden. Covert narcissists can often just seem like a bit of an insensitive person, ignoring your needs, belittling you, and having no regard for your feelings. They tend towards depression. They are extremely sensitive to criticism, and capable of a great deal of self-sacrifice. They use their suffering and victimhood to keep people chained to them, and they have a particular talent for binding extremely sensitive people to them, precisely because of that victimhood status. Sensitive people tend to be compassionate, and often labor under the illusion that it is our duty to help loved ones who have suffered great trauma, even in the face of their continual abuse and our own continual suffering. We excuse their bad behavior with the flawed perception that it is just a result of their trauma, and because we are so strong, it is no big deal.

This is particularly the case for people who have historically endured intense oppression, like women. If the person with NPD has ever supported us or provided for our needs (like a mother) this is especially true, and it is easy to adopt a position of indebtedness. I have always noticed that covert narcissists, who are almost always female, are surrounded by kind, sensitive people who help uphold the illusion they have created of themselves as these battle-worn warriors who have persevered despite all odds. Everyone around them is usually pretty well-versed in all the ways that the covert narcissist has suffered, so their loved ones are usually focused more on the suffering of the covert narcissist than on the suffering they are causing everyone around them. With the covert narcissist, the outward high self-esteem has shifted to outward low self-esteem, simply because this garners sympathy, protection, and wins you friends and thus influence over others.

This is where the final sentence earlier in my interpretation of the DSM definition of narcissism applies: Covert narcissists will pretend to be whatever they need to be, and whatever they are allowed to be in limited circumstances, to have power and influence over others. They are the victim turned hero having become a champion for victims' rights. Covert narcissists are created from a world that makes it very difficult for certain groups (like women) to be in public positions of power, so that empowerment that everyone needs to feel internally has to be located in more private areas and is more hidden. An example of this is the fact that women usually murder someone they know well or are related to. Since women have been so often restricted to the roles of wife and mother, they have historically mainly had power in the home, so this is where women have wielded their power either positively or negatively depending on their level of mental health. The case of Gabriel Fernandez, the little boy who was brutally murdered by his mother and her boyfriend in Los Angeles, CA, is a perfect example of how horrific a narcissistic woman can be—and par for the course, the mother was severely abused as a child as well[14].

It is easy for so many of us to point to the history of women's oppression, but not so easy to acknowledge some of the horrific outcomes of this oppression. Many of the destructive patterns that have emerged in women, like addiction and depression, are a result of these circumstances of being so limited in self-expression. Covert narcissism is another outcome. When you have been subjected to abuse, and you cannot create your self-worth as CEO, sports star, or leader of a nation, you will resort to the areas you are allowed into, which for women have been either based on their sexuality, or their roles as nurturers and caretakers. This is exquisitely revealed in many episodes of *Deadly Women*, the popular show on I.D. television network since 2005. Almost all the female murderers on that show kill either spouses or children. Season 7, Episode 9 *'Above the Law'* includes the story of probably one of the most infamous serial killers in history (male or female), Dorothy Tann.

The section was mainly narrated by the author of *The Baby Thief* (2007) Barbara Bisantz Raymond, and told the story of Dorothy Tann, who ran an orphanage in Memphis, Tennessee in the 1940's. She over-saw decades of adoptions and by the age of 49 was known as the mother of modern adoption—a practice that was apparently very uncommon prior to the 1920's. Tann's orphanage was utilized by many Hollywood stars, including the afore-mentioned Joan Crawford, and she was well-respected by politicians, doctors, judges and even presidents; President Truman invited her to his inauguration and Eleanor Roosevelt consulted her regarding child welfare[15]. Tann's orphanage operated for over 30 years and she was a millionaire by the time she died, after which it was discovered that she had been stealing babies from widows, poor or unwed women, and that by the time of her death, she had caused the death of an estimated 500 babies[16]! She hired women called 'baby pickers' to go to poor neighborhoods and claim to be taking a baby to get healthcare if they were sick, never returning and telling the mother that the baby had died. Deaths occurred from neglect, like providing no medicine to sick babies, or leaving those who were not adopted out in the sun to bake; the infant mortality rate in Memphis became the highest in the nation, and despite many parents reporting her to authorities, they were ignored because she had so many officials in her pocket[17]. Eventual reports from the women who worked with her confirmed a cruel, sadistic personality.

Covert narcissist and serial killer Aileen Wuornos became a prostitute after a tragically negligent and abusive childhood and used her position to eventually go on a killing spree, murdering multiple men after providing them with sexual services. Because she had been raped and abused by so many men, she convinced herself that her actions were righteous, and even a result of self-defense. Her victim-hood status morphed into a predatorial nature, and she lost all empathy for men who engaged with prostitutes, seeing them only as raging beasts who needed to be brought down. Joan Crawford, the star of autobiographical film *Mommie Dearest* (1981), adopted children whom she violently abused behind closed doors because they were not her 'fans' and did not lavish her with praise like her adoring public. She thought that motherhood was a role that would garnish her positive attention, but soon found that it required more self-sacrifice and patience than she was capable of.

There is always so much chaos, drama, and tension around covert narcissists, mainly because of another main characteristic, which is extreme sensitivity. They cannot bear for you to ask them to do something in a different way, or not do something for a reason they may be innocently unaware of. It is a massive personal slight to them for you to ask them to adjust their behavior. I see it affect them immediately. Either they get quiet and terse, and then say something mean to you at a totally different time because they've just been waiting to get you back, or they point out something you've done wrong, and try to shift the blame. Either way, they turn very small issues requiring a very basic level of modification or cooperation, which every human being who shares a living space must do, into mountains. When you alert them to something in their behavior or actions that may be causing some conflict or discomfort for someone else, they take it as a complete affront to them, a huge criticism, and it affects them deeply because they are very invested in an identity with no flaws.

Which particular flaw depends on the person; some could be invested in keeping their house clean and beautiful, some in the lives of their children, some in their good looks. If you appear to have any kind of problem with their housekeeping, child, or appearance, it wounds them deeply. They are hurt, they feel the hurt deeply, and they begin to feel other things that go along with hurt like pain, resentment, and anger. They then begin to radiate this resentment and anger from their very core and behave in ways that make it clear they are not happy. But it's all very subtle and just builds and builds over time until everyone is stressed out and nobody has any idea why because it's been 100 little things over time; little ways that coverts insist on always having their way and doing things the way they want it done, regardless of it making no sense or not being the most efficient method. They will not consider any flaws in their opinions or any self-centeredness in their behavior. They expect everyone to constantly adjust to them, because they need to reinforce their image as powerful and smart every single day.

They try to reinforce others' adjustment to them with gifts or the reward of their own temporary happiness, and when people stop constantly adjusting, they sulk, pout, and mope around like no one loves them. I think the key to them getting away with this is the intermittent reward they provide when they do get what they want. From time to time, they seem happy and animated, so it makes it seem like you are just, you know, having a relationship! There are ups and downs, and it's normal. Except that the downs are inevitable, because it's a game. It's the covert narcissists' personal movie of conquering the world and constantly proving their strength, superiority, and intelligence.

It's exhausting. They will drain the very life out of you, and then they will apologize to keep you around once everyone else has abandoned them, and you then have to take care of your abuser. I have seen so many mothers do this to their children, and children have very little defense against an emotionally manipulative mother. You simply absolutely believe you must stay by her side, and of course you really want to, and the covert narcissist KNOWS this about you. So, they will act whatever part they need to act to keep you around, including being repentant.

The thing is, what all narcissists really want is power, because they were made to feel so powerless at some point. They will get that power wherever and however they can. Because of how we are socialized, this will manifest differently in people based on where they have access to power. Men have traditionally been valued for things like being courageous, strong, brave, skilled, wealthy, and entrepreneurial. You know, President. Women have traditionally been valued more for being nurturing, caring, supportive, compassionate, organized, beautiful, and diplomatic. This means that women have influence and power over the people who are attracted to them, or those they take care of. The identity that is often created by female covert narcissists is one of the matriarch taking care of everyone's needs, and eventually having to neglect their own needs in this process. The dysfunction created from this type of suffering is expressed through the covert narcissist as a persistent need for acknowledgment, control, and influence over others. Absolute power. This is because they feel they never received those things. They have suffered and you owe them. You should have no problems with doing things for them that cause you discomfort because they have suffered so much discomfort for you and others.

Now what I am describing is actually mainly the private experience with a covert narcissist. Many of them are able to maintain a public persona of one who is caring, empathetic, dutiful, and very tough. An example is the mother with Munchausen Syndrome who can easily shed tears and appear to be in distress over someone's else's suffering, which they are secretly causing. This is a dangerously destructive personality. Being in the position of nurse or mother can be easily utilized to get the help, support, and recognition that was never supplied by those who were the narcissists' caretakers when they were a child.

This type of recognition is especially plentiful from compassionate, caring folk who recognize the unfairness of what the covert narcissist has been through in their childhood or is presently going through. And believe me, they will tell you all about it! They will constantly share the stories of all their suffering and abuse and how unfair life has always been and how unfairly they have always been treated. They are the quintessential victim, and they can easily be led to tears if you ever have the slightest problem with them. It is your duty to put up with their terrible treatment of you because after all, they can't help it. They are like this because of what was done to them and they just need help to get better. This my friends, is where you, the compassionate caring person comes in.

Chapter 2

THE EXPERIENCE

Introduction

For over 30 years now, I have suffered from hip and sciatica pain, which is probably a long-term result of an injury I acquired doing gymnastics which was never treated. I had very lofty dreams of going to the Olympics and had a huge picture of Nadia Comaneci on my wall. I had been taking gymnastics for many years, and one day when I was 12 in the 7th grade, I swung around the top bar of the uneven parallel bars and as a result of someone re-adjusting the lower bar for their height (everyone was taller than me), smashed my pelvis bone instead of my stomach muscles into the bar. I blacked out immediately and could barely walk when I regained consciousness. I was sent home, or rather, to the one of about four houses we had lived in that year. My mother told her good friend whom I was staying with (my mother was out of town) that I was faking it and just didn't want to go to school. I couldn't walk for about three days, and afterwards eventually had to give up my beloved gymnastics, which I had been doing since I was five years old. My right leg could no longer take the pressure of landing and jumping, and frankly, I became really afraid of being injured after that—in fact, paralyzed with fear. Years before, my mother took me to a chiropractor because I was having back pain, and he informed her that I was born with slight scoliosis and spina bifida and that I should probably wear a back brace for a short period of time, but that never happened, so that may have exacerbated the injury.

I also had various dental problems that were never treated (a tooth actually turned black) and I am having problems with gum and jaw pain to this day. The only injury I was ever treated for (and there were many because I am a klutz), was my broken wrist, but it took hours for my stepfather to get me to the hospital. We had one of those typical orange hippie-vans with the tie-dyed curtains and all. The sliding door to get into the back was very heavy and had to be shut really hard. As we were pulling off from the Health Food store in the West End, I slammed the door as hard as I could, but it didn't shut. My stepfather took off really fast, and before I could get my hand out of the handle, the door flew back slamming my elbow into some metal object protruding out from the door slot, and my wrist bent all the way back to my arm which got caught between the door and the car, cracking it quite quickly. The pain was so intense I just passed out on the floor of the van. My stepfather just drove around, running errands, while I lay on the floor of the van bleeding out from the hole in my elbow for about 3 hours before taking me to the hospital.

So, I did not get much medical care as a child. I spent a lot of time alone, which honestly, I preferred. At least I wasn't getting yelled at, punished, or hit … this was also partly because I was a latch-key kid by the time I was five. I would be home for many hours by myself. The first traumatic experience I can really remember was when I was five years old. I was home alone after school trying to make toast for a snack, and then watch Sesame Street. I felt somewhat guilty because I hadn't finished my homework yet, but I just really loved Sesame Street! Cookie Monster was my man. The toaster was busted, and the bread had to be manually popped out of the slots. After I dropped each slice in, I went to the living room to try to turn on the TV. It was on the top shelf of a bookshelf that was unfortunately not nailed to the wall, and most likely leaning over a bit, and as I climbed up onto the 2nd shelf to reach the power knob, the whole thing toppled over on me—knocked me out cold! I don't know how long I laid there, but I came-to in a smoke-filled house to the sound of someone calling my name. The downstairs neighbor, Ms. Jackson, had noticed the smoke coming through the vents, and came upstairs and banged on the front door of our apartment until I regained consciousness.

God Bless her. We really underestimate the physical danger that young children are in when they aren't properly supervised. Kids just don't understand gravity yet. Another horrible memory I have is baby-sitting my little sister when I was about 8 and she was 1 and she somehow got out the back door and busted her head open on one of the concrete steps. I got in tremendous trouble for that and felt horrible about it for years.

Now on top of the danger, there was absolutely no stability. I counted once that we moved about 11 times through-out my childhood to 4 different states, that I attended about 10 different schools, and that my mother had about 28 different boyfriends by the time I finished college. I put all the names I could remember on a list once ... the one who stayed the longest and who I refer to as my stepfather because it is my sister's father, was with us from the time I was about 7 until 14. I believe he also has NPD.

His motus operandi was rage. He was very violent and was physically abusive to all three of us (me, my little sister and my mother) from time to time. He had a terrible, violent temper. He was always kicking in doors, busting mirrors, and generally raging about. But even he didn't physically abuse me as much as my mother did. It was worse because he was stronger, but it was not as often. My mother was always slapping me, pinching me, or popping me in the middle of my forehead, and I was constantly threatened with violence and punishment.

Now these days, I must say I hear this from comedians all the time, and a lot of them seem to still really love their parent(s), I am assuming partly because they have a sense of something they were doing wrong that deserved to be corrected. I get that. And while I don't support punishing children with violence, having helped raise twin boys myself, I am aware that some kids are not the docile creature I was as a child. To put this in perspective, my mother told me that at 7 months, I could be put on a blanket in the grass and just sit there quietly while she hung clothes up to dry. My memory of myself and the feedback I have received from other adults and family is that I was a very calm, well-behaved child. People have told me they

LOVED to baby-sit me because I always made the bed, folded my clothes neatly, and was very tidy. I always got good grades, never got in trouble, and basically did as I was told. It is thus very difficult for me to remember what any of the physical violence that my mother subjected me to was about. I do recall that some of it was for lying, or eating candy, or lying about eating candy! My mother had very strong opinions about food. But for the most part, I cannot recall what I had ever done that seemed punishment worthy—particularly violent punishment. This is especially true now that I have raised my own child.

Anyway, my sister's father was cray-cray. Once he left me and my little sister at a summer camp for hours after everyone had gone home, and a kindly cafeteria worker stayed behind so that we wouldn't be alone. I was about 10 and my sister was around 3. She got thirsty and the lady told us there was some peach juice she could have. My stepfather showed up at the moment my sister took her first sip and flew into a rage when he tasted her drink and determined it was punch and not juice. He told me all the way home in the car that I was going to GET it. I was terrified. And he did indeed whup my ass. He would leave scars on my legs from the switch and I would be too ashamed to play outside for days.

The man was just always angry, or on the other hand, quite jovial and fun so THAT was confusing as shit. He is the one that took us to the park, out for ice-cream, and to hang out with friends and watch basketball. He stayed in my life for years after he and my mom separated because of my relationship with my sister. The energy from him over the years just got creepier and creepier … he was actually on *The Oprah Winfrey Show* (1986) once many years ago, representing an organization out of the Bay Area in Cali that assisted men who had been guilty of domestic violence. Seeing that show was a real out-of-this-universe, bizzarro-world, The-Upside-Down type of experience. He was going on and on about how to help men not be violent, how to manage their rage and such, and never once did he say that he had been an abuser as well. That was when I learned not to believe everything you see on TV, and at the age of 17 or so, that was a good lesson.

He apparently went on to abuse his next girlfriend after splitting from my mom—I remember a story of him choking her over a bannister. Once my mother had to call the Oakland Police because she was on the phone with my sister as her dad had his hands wrapped around her throat choking her as well. They had gotten into a huge fight. She was dating her first love (who also happened to sell drugs) and apparently, she had threatened to have her father killed while going off on him in the middle of her own rage. I am sure she would never have done it—but it was drama. Her father and his girlfriend had pretty much let my sister have an entire apartment on Lake Merritt to herself at the age of 16. Yeah. While dating a drug-dealer. Whose father had also been a drug-dealer. So, no boundaries, no guidance, no real parenting was happening while she was at a very impressionable age.

You know, just to share the curious multi-dimensionality of human beings, her boyfriend was actually a really special person. I remember her telling me a story about him finding his goldfish dead and bringing it back to life by shocking it with two electrical wires! When I met him, he seemed so intelligent and thoughtful ... ah the greatness many of our young men could have achieved if they had not developed in such violent and destructive environments ... anyway, my sister really struggled so much in her youth, and it pained me to see her suffering the fate of having two very damaged human beings as parents. But I understand that this is a fate many of us suffer to varying degrees. There are so many negative repercussions on children raised by people who were abused themselves.

One of them for me was that I wet the bed until I was about 13. I was usually severely scolded and punished for it. I always felt so ashamed. I would literally be having dreams of going to the bathroom and thinking I was on the toilet. I was viciously afraid of the dark and I believed monsters were under my bed, so I was terrified to get up in the middle of the night to go urinate. I would hold it and go to sleep, and my body was like uh-uh. It's so crazy to remember now how terrified I was thinking that hands were going to reach out from under the bed and grab my ankles! Oh the nightmares ... my days and nights were filled with terror. And nobody knew. Everyone thought we were the perfect little family.

My mother was very ahead of her time in terms of understanding health and nutrition. She got her Ph.D. and wrote her dissertation on the politics of health care in America in the late 70's - early 80's, long before it was really a public discussion. This is amazing to me now in light of the health-care disaster we are facing. She really was ahead of her time. She would not get me vaccinated. She would not use over-the counter medicines at ALL. She was all, 'fuck processed food, sugar and pharmaceuticals'—in the 70's!

Unfortunately, what this meant for the extreme, intense, narcissistic personality that she was, is that she believed most food was toxic, and she would never feed me while we were out and about because nothing was healthy enough. Keep in mind the health-food industry was nowhere NEAR as commercial as it is now. There was no Whole Foods. I would be salivating at the food at people's houses that they always offered, but that I could not have. I would be in the back seat of our car, starving, weak, and listless after running around with her for hours and hours. She would get angry with me and accuse me of being an attention hound, or of trying to be pathetic to get sympathy. I have been battling a severe eating disorder my entire life.

She would though, be very attentive to me when I had a cold or the flu. I do believe that I slowly developed a pre-disposition towards illness because it was the only time she was nurturing or caring with me. She was often away from home to attend conferences, lectures, teach classes, or whatever else her job as a professor required, so I grew up very fast. I learned how to cook, clean, and take care of my little sister from a very young age. I had my first job at 12. I was an assistant in a holistic doctor's office. I worked at Taco Bell when I was 14. I worked at a Health Food store when I was 16. I had a job every summer during college and went straight to work on Wall Street in New York once I graduated.

I used a lot of intoxicants in college! I went on a straight-up alcohol, weed, and LSD binge my first week in college because I was euphoric over having escaped my home. I fell in love almost immediately with a guy who was probably consistently cheating on me, and the heartbreaks from relationships have been non-stop ever since. I mean NON-STOP. Looking back now, I realize I had horRIfic experiences ... I thought I was dying when I lost my virginity. I was 16 and hadn't even gotten my period yet. I was so in love with the boy; I mean obsessively-followed him around school-still know his phone number to this day, desperately in love! After having sex with him, I bled non-stop for about a month, and had to lie to my mom and tell her I had started my period so I could get sanitary napkins. I seriously thought that I was going to die. He never called me, and when I returned to school after Christmas break, he already had another girlfriend. I have walked in on a boyfriend and another lover several times, been date raped, stolen from (Yeah I am talking to YOU Martin who stole my The Family album with *Screams of Passion* (1996) on it!); I guess just your basic plethora of being used and abused when I was just stupidly but desperately searching for love. I have had no idea how to pick someone truly compatible with me, and I never had anyone in my life with any wisdom to just give me the basic in's and out's about sex and being young and how predatorial people can be.

I completely broke down about a year after I graduated from college. I was living in New York, working on Wall Street at J.P. Morgan as a permanent temp (yeah figure that out!), and pursuing my passions for acting and music, but was not taking care of myself at all. As I said, those years of being starved had led me to an eating disorder and I was accomplishing a great deal, but not eating much or drinking enough water. Pizza, bagels, and red wine was my diet. Cheap food is a necessity when your entire paycheck goes to rent, bills, train, laundry, and toiletries. But I was doing well! I got on the cover of a magazine, an ABC children's television show, and recorded music with a band signed to Polygram Records. I was doing it. I worked during the day and performed at night and on the weekends. I eventually lost about 20 lbs. and started getting really bad bladder and urinary tract infections. I swear to you I literally pissed on my myself walking home on Atlantic Ave. in Brooklyn, thanking GOD it was dark and praying no one was in the lobby of my building. It was probably a result of all the red wine I was drinking on an empty stomach. I eventually woke up one morning after about a year of this and could not move.

The health problems have been numerous ever since and for the last 25 years. Only recently, at the age of almost 50, have I finally been able to enjoy basic good health. I have utilized pretty much every medical treatment that exists to heal my illnesses including pharmaceuticals, surgery and other various procedures, acupuncture, herbs, hypnotism, chiropractic treatment, and homeopathics. You name it, I've tried it. I have suffered from intense sciatica pain that has literally kept me from walking at times for at least 20 years, urinary tract and kidney infections that would cause me to pee blood, intestinal issues that eventually led to celiac's disease, and every female problem there is including fibroid tumors, ovarian cysts, endometriosis, PID, and bacterial infections. But the worst of all, is that I have battled severe depression for years. I never took anti-depressants, so I have basically been living with suicidal thoughts for most of my life.

If you have experienced these things—constant health problems, depression, illnesses, chronic pain and fatigue, difficulty in romantic relationships, and what feels like constant, unbearable, severe heartbreak, chances are you grew up with a narcissist. It is impossible to grow up with a narcissist and not suffer to some degree, because the environment that they create is so toxic. It is unhealthy for them and everyone involved. It is a constant storm of chaos, conflict, instability, fear, anger, violence, sickness, emergencies, sadness, blame, guilt, manipulation, lies, and deceit. There is very little optimism, hope, support, acknowledgment, nurturing, encouragement, or wisdom and guidance.

Now the tricky thing is, and this is especially true of the covert narcissist, it doesn't mean that there aren't good times. My mother was also a very warm, affectionate, funny, down to earth person who on top of everything was absolutely brilliant. I learned so much from her. She had the very first reggae program on WRFG radio in Atlanta and would play my favorite song by Bob Marley, *No Woman No Cry* (1974) every Sunday when she was on the air. We always had a lot of books, a lot of good music, and I was forced to participate in many, many enriching experiences. I saw lots of dance, music and theater. We had phenomenal writers like Toni Cade Bambara, Ntozake Shange, and Olivia Butler to our house for dinner. Our bookshelves were filled with everything from Eastern Spirituality, to Howard Zinn, to Frank Herbert, to Charles Dickens. Our music collection included John Coltrane, Billie Holiday, Sarah Vaughn, Ella Fitzgerald, Duke Ellington, Miles Davis, The Beatles, Janis Joplin, Jimi Hendrix, Blood Sweat & Tears, Bobbie Blue Bland, Esther Phillips, Earth Wind & Fire, The Blackbyrds, James Brown, Chaka Khan, Stevie Wonder, Donnie Hathaway—you get the picture. Our walls were covered with posters of Nelson Mandela, Mao Tse Tung, Bob Marley, and Africa, Africa, Africa. My mother believed in supporting the arts and most definitely wanted me to be an informed and intelligent young woman. She was an amazing artist herself. She had these secret lovely pencil drawings on canvas in the back of a closet in her office. She was a feminist and a revolutionary and an incredible writer, and I was pushed to be a very high achiever which served me well in life as I was always able to support myself with numerous skills. She was also an amazing cook! She was especially good at baking and made the most delicious vegetarian chocolate chip cookies, zucchini bread, and even doughnuts. She told me once that she was actually given the name most people know her by because she used to bake bread for people in college and the name she was given meant 'bread' in an African language.

But all the positives were conditional. If she was not in a good mood, which was the majority of the time, the narcissist lurking within was always ready and waiting to emerge, and no one knew but me. My sister was too young to really know what was going on, and the face my mother put on for the outside world was just a completely different personality than what we were experiencing at home.

What made it really difficult is that in the Black American community, revolutionaries are held in high-esteem—like Malcolm X or Angela Davis. Because of this, very few people from my childhood are willing to accept who my mother was behind closed doors. She was seen as a hero, and many people were and still are completely unwilling to see her any other way. I am aware of many, many students whose lives she touched deeply, especially when she became provost of a popular university. She actually wrote a poem about the history of slavery in America that is carved into a beautiful monument in Jamestown, Virginia. Her public persona has always been one of a progressive genius. This has also been supported by my sister actively up-holding that image—just FYI, narcissists always have family members that are on their side no matter what.

The ironic thing is that my sister was much more reactionary to my mother's abusive treatment than I was; she would meet her violence with violence. I was much too afraid and would never even consider that I could hit my mother back. Or set fire to a box of her research ... yep, that happened! My sister did not take the physical abuse the way I did, and I think the outcome is that my mother was just much more psychologically manipulative with her. Well, to put it bluntly, she just lied to my sister and my sister believed the lies. We were seven years apart, so it was a case of my word against my mother's. I didn't have any money, so it was also much more convenient to be on my mother's side! My mother had adjusted her behavior to support her public image, and she had started making more money after I went off to college, so she was able to do more financially for my sister. My sister was also just so sweet and sensitive. We had so many good times together when we were young. She was even there at the birth of my child …

As a child, this type of behavior and treatment from a parent is an almost impossible thing to comprehend and respond to in a way that protects you. Children have very basic needs, but they are non-negotiable. Just as you cannot live without air, food, and water, human beings cannot thrive without healthy inter-connection, self-sufficiency, and a sense of self-value. These things are achieved through nurturing, support, understanding, and compassion. It is a foundation of basic psychology as agreed upon by everyone from Freud to Erickson[1], that if human beings do not receive and experience these things, they will attempt to get and experience them in a myriad of healthy and unhealthy ways until they die.

Essentially, when you are raised by a narcissist, you are developing in the environment of someone who did not get what they needed as a child, so they have no idea how to give you what you need. It is really difficult when it is a covert narcissist, because you are dealing with the extreme multi-dimensionality of a human being who has achieved so many amazing things in the world and who others see as a straight-up hero as a result of their good works, so you are living in this weird matrix where the experience you are having with this person is completely different from what others are experiencing with them. Your reality is that you are trapped in the personal movie of someone who approaches life in general in multiple dysfunctional ways. They are constantly caught up in soap-opera-like drama in all their relationships as a result of trying to control everyone and everything. It is dizzying.

Because ultimately, we have absolutely no control over others, and no amount of control over the external world is ever an adequate substitute for the base-line sense of comfort a person with healthy self-esteem has, and this is something that should have been slowly developing internally through-out childhood. And there are oh so many ways we can go about feeling something that is close to healthy self-esteem! Sex, love, drugs, food, accomplishments, money, fame—these are all things that give you an immediate good feeling, but the problem is that it never lasts because that feeling isn't fully integrated into you, it is just a temporary experience. If as a child you are developing around people who mainly pursue temporary 'good feeling-fixes' to manage stress, you will never know what to do to actually achieve good feelings in an internal, and mainly permanent way. Temporary fixes include alcohol, bullying, and even setting and achieving goals. The lack of good feeling, or high self-esteem, leads to a type of life-long internal stress and has been discovered by many doctors and scientists alike now to be the foundation of life-long mental and physical illnesses. You can literally have a broken heart. It has been determined through vast research that abused and/or neglected children have higher rates of all the worst mental and physical illnesses including heart disease, diabetes, cancer, depression, and anxiety[2].

To be clear, not all narcissists are physically abusive—which may actually be a worse situation in some ways because it makes it much more difficult for the victim of the narcissist to really be able to see the truth about them. Many narcissists are extremely verbally abusive, and this can mess up a child's psyche so bad, that they are never able to believe anything good about themselves and they continue to be the victim of other predators. I personally have a very close friend whose father is a bona-fide narcissist and while he didn't physically abuse him, he consistently verbally abused him through-out his childhood. I was there, so I am not speaking second hand. He would always call him stupid, a donkey, and a dumb ass. This friend of mine can fix cars, build engines, grow gardens with the most beautiful vegetables, cook his ass off, build bathrooms and even entire houses, and has a vast knowledge of herbs and medicine. He is an extremely knowledgeable and skilled person, but has struggled his entire life with addiction, depression, and chronic pain. I have another very good friend whose mother didn't physically or verbally abuse her, but she constantly manipulated her, lied to her, neglected her health needs (which were crucial because she had heart-surgery as an infant), and pretty much created a toxic environment for both her and her sister, which has eventually led to her sister developing severe mental illness and constantly attempting suicide. I can tell you myself that as hurtful as the beatings were, the life-long scars I struggle with the most have been a result of the neglect, the verbal and emotional abuse, and the constant belittling.

I am always amazed at how one, lone, narcissistic individual can cause so much damage to so many people. They generally cause mayhem and chaos in the lives of everyone in their immediate environment, and they will appear to be just fine while everyone else is suffering tremendously.

The covert narcissist is extra EXTRA brilliant at this because they have everyone convinced that they are this wonderful, self-sacrificing saint whose mission in life is to help humanity and save the less fortunate and the victims, when what they really are is a total opportunist obsessed with their image. Every 'good' thing they do is in the public eye, but behind closed doors they are emotional tyrants.

If you have constantly heard phrases like "how dare you!" or "Oh we just had a misunderstanding" in situations where you have felt hurt or used, chances are you were interacting with a covert narcissist. There are constantly misunderstandings, confusion, and major problems with communication. It is usually when you try to stand up for yourself and try desperately to get the narcissist to listen to you that you will hear things like "no one else has this issue with me" or "you are mistaken, that didn't happen." They deny, deny, deny. It can make you feel crazy. Let's talk about the lies!

The Lies

To call those with NPD liars is an understatement of epic proportions. They are basically pathoLOGICAL liars. I am often of the mind that they don't know how to tell the truth. They tell so many lies all the time that it is very difficult for most normal, decent people to fathom that someone would lie that much, and often right to your face. It just doesn't seem possible to those of us that are mainly honest. I mean, everyone tells those little lies now and then to varying degrees for decorum or security, or even self-protection, and this is what really helps to give narcissists a sort of secret power to enforce lies.

The secret Jedi Mind Trick that narcissists use is that they always mix in a little bit of the truth. This makes people reluctant to believe that the majority of what they say are lies, because if you know that some of what they are saying is true, then a part of you, especially when you are young, assumes "well, the rest is probably true as well." I believe I heard someone estimate in an interview I saw recently that Donald Trump had told approximately 20,000 lies to date[3] (that there is a body of people fact-checking his statements and counting the lies should say everything you need to know about this poster child for NPD). When I became an adult, the number of lies that I was able to identify that my mother told me was just astounding. I had entire versions of stories from her life completely wrong. She had told me things about my father and their relationship that were totally fabricated, and the truth changed my entire view about the situation.

Most of my life I thought that my father, who was an ex-Black Panther/RNA member and a self-proclaimed revolutionary, had hijacked an airplane to Cuba after an attempt to free a fellow comrade from jail, leaving his loving wife and baby to be a martyr for the cause of the liberation of people of color, that he and my mother were in love, and that she had failed at her attempt to join him and re-unite our family, instead falling into the position of one of the unfortunate casualties of the Black Civil Rights era in America. This was my reality for 23 years. I had met other Panther children and had been in the company of many well-known revolutionaries such as Kathleen Cleaver, Jamal Joseph, and Assata Shakur, all of whom are beautiful souls. My whole childhood was about Black people's struggle for freedom and the fight against oppressive White America. The reality of this particular situation made it very difficult for me to see my mom as anything else but a hero. My entire life narrative was that my mother was a victim of oppression who remained strong under tyranny and triumphed in the end with the sheer power of her intellect and fighting spirit. When I visited my father in Havana the 2nd time and on my own at the age of 23 (I was with my mother the first time I met him) I found out the real story.

The truth was that they had split up some time before he had hijacked the plane, in part because she had pulled a shotgun on him and threatened to shoot him. This was a revelation! The most important factor in this revelation was that this violent streak she had consistently shown me was not a result of the trauma from the loss of a beloved husband and the ensuing struggle as a single mother, but a part of her make-up since I was an infant. My father was a very truthful person, sometimes too much, and he assured me he had not laid a hand on her, had not cheated on her, and was basically just intent on carrying out the actions that eventually led him to hijacking an airplane to Cuba, but that is another story ...

Many of the lies that narcissists tell are often justifiable reasons behind why they are the way they are or have done the things they have done that are obviously harmful to others. There is always this idea that they are a victim of unfortunate familial or societal circumstances, and that they should be given a pass for the terrible things they do because after all, they are damaged and hurt and have done the best they could in challenging circumstances.

In my case there was also the powerful narrative of racist America, the oppression of women, and the suffering of the impoverished. This narrative is one that is true for many, many Black folk, and it makes it very challenging to say the least, to see past your image of a loved one as a hero, to the reality of their personality disorder. As life moves on however, one often finds that these personality traits, which often include a proclivity to violence, tyrannical behavior, and an incessant need for attention were all present in the narcissist from a very young age.

Now, aside from all the grandiose lies narcissists will tell you about their suffering, or in the case of overt narcissists, their accomplishments, they also constantly just tell little lies on a daily basis to their loved ones. Sometimes I have wondered like, why lie about that? They never want to take the blame for anything, own up to any bad habits or mistakes, or take responsibility for a misunderstanding. They blame everything on everyone else, and project all of their emotions onto others.

One of the very deleterious consequences of this is what is referred to as triangulation or splitting. In popular culture it has been referred to as 'divide and conquer.' They will secretly pit their loved ones against each other by telling everyone lies about each other. I have come to the conclusion over the years that the purpose of the lies is just to get their way all the time, or to have influence over the people who love them, or really quite often, to cover the tracks of the unethical or sloppy stuff they do. Now I think that mainly they just don't want to look bad.

For example, if they have spent too much money on things they want, they will project to each of two people they are working with that it was the other who is responsible in some way for why the finances are dwindling. No one knows what is going on for years because there is so little trust between them that everyone just clams up, doesn't talk to one another, and carries on in a covert manner, believing that the 'other' is out to get them or manipulate them because of what the narcissist has told them. Narcissists will also get people to aid them unknowingly in getting their way by not telling whoever is helping them at the time what is really going on, and making the other person think that the person helping the narcissist is on the side of the narcissist. When all is said and done, much will be destroyed and/or lost, like a business or a home, and it may take years for everyone to sort out all the lies they have been told and determine that they have all been duped.

Narcissists will throw EVERYONE under the bus. Even their own children. Just take a look at what happened to numerous Donald Trump colleagues … I fear for Ivanka … though she is so thoroughly participating in her father's madness, that I guess we can all only have so much sympathy for her when his house of cards comes crashing down. And I promise you people, it will come crashing down. One very important thing to understand about narcissists is that they are on a slowly sinking boat, and if you are riding with them, you will surely drown along with them—and often long before them.

The Outcome

Why is it a sinking boat? This is inherently connected to the idea that they actually do not have high self-esteem, but in fact very low self-esteem. One of the most important pieces of evidence in a person's life that points to how much they value themselves, are the choices they make. If you don't want to be sick, you will not eat something rotten. If you don't want to die in a car crash, you will wear your seatbelt. If you don't want to be homeless, you will dedicate the appropriate energy towards finding ways to support yourself and maintain a balanced life. When you like yourself, simply put, you will want to live a joyful, healthy life. Now on the other side of that, if you care very little for yourself and your life, you will probably make choices that reflect this. Believe me I know! I did it for years. I starved myself, stayed in abusive relationships, and kept going back to the most abusive person, my mother, out of a need for love.

Of course, I know it isn't completely this simple. There are numerous biological and environmental factors like addiction, conditioning, and a lack of knowledge that lead to people making destructive choices. So much of our motivations are being fueled by our subconscious and those nasty voices in our head that are so full of fear and trauma. Even in these instances though, if someone really wants to find peace and happiness, they will make an effort to learn from their mistakes and grow and evolve. Unfortunately, this often means losing people, and the simple fact is that most of don't want to feel alone and unloved.

One of the main challenges to this concept of making sound choices, is the concept of immediate gratification versus delayed gratification. The science of these two choices is that the former is generally very temporary, and the latter is more long-term and often permanent. America's opioid epidemic is a perfect example of this. Numbing your pain provides temporary relief in the moment, but continuing this practice beyond the prescribed 3 to 6 months that good doctors (like Dr. Oz) submit for how long someone should take a pain-killer, will cause eventual serious health complications and clearly, even death. Exercising may immediately cause you muscle soreness and fatigue, but if continued will create a foundation for long-lasting and even permanent good health. It can absolutely be tricky trying to determine what are the things that will cause eventual problems, and what are the things that even if unpleasant in the moment, will create long-term advantages.

I can tell you that narcissists consistently make choices that will inevitably lead to their destruction. This is because they are generally pulled towards instant gratification, and anything that will make them feel good immediately—investments that will yield immediate results, expenditures that will make them look good, and purchases that will exaggerate their external worth. Whether or not the acquisitions are actually well-made, will quickly diminish in value, or cause the pain and suffering of others is never a consideration. Narcissists want what they want when they want it, and the future is rarely considered. This is what creates a sinking boat. The narcissist's boat is always built on a shaky foundation. Here's why: What makes a nation, a family, any group strong? The people that it is made of. Strong, healthy, capable people create a formidable group. A group made of damaged, weak, traumatized people cannot get much done and will probably eventually collapse. They will create an unhealthy atmosphere and circumstances that will eventually crumble. Like Rome. Like cults. Like corrupt companies. Like greedy politicians. Therefore, all decisions that lead to other people's downfall will eventually lead to the person's downfall who is making those decisions.

Think of narcissists Caligula, Mussolini, and Ted Bundy. Murt, murt, and murt. Killed in horrific ways.

Decisions that provide for long-term and social well-being may present circumstances that are challenging, such as how a mother may put aside her own needs to provide what her children need, but those children will more than likely grow up to be strong and then they will be able to provide for their mother's needs so that she can truly enjoy the remainder of her life. Doing good for others almost inevitably leads to others wanting to do good for you (unless you are doing good for someone with NPD). But if you consistently make decisions that cause other's discomfort and pain, like with the decisions made in Vietnam, or in our health-care system, you create a situation that produces a war veteran who may lose his mind and attack or kill his loved ones, or a nation full of obese and drug addicted citizens. Very few people on a sinking boat will live, because the sharks will come. The main point I am making though, is that the Captain of the boat will go down with it. It may take a while to manifest as with the legacy of Leo Baekland, the creator of plastic, which is the most toxic substance ever made, and how his grandson murdered his own mother and then eventually committed suicide by suffocating himself with a plastic bag (seriously!)[4]. Or it may happen quickly like with the murder of Caligula, one of the worst narcissists that has ever lived. Narcissist are always making decisions that put other people at risk or in danger because they don't truly care about anyone.

Something I have been saying for years, is that a narcissist will kill you. It may happen suddenly, or it may occur slowly and over a long period of time. I have seen many people succumb to mental or physical illness as a result of prolonged narcissistic abuse, and die. If you are deeply connected in an emotional relationship with a narcissist, you will suffer, because they are suffering. While it may seem like external factors are the cause of their suffering, I promise you, it is all coming from within them. They are tortured souls who never healed their wounds and are raging through life, burning bridges and leaving charred souls in the wake of their destructive behavior.

The reason you will suffer is because we are all connected. This isn't just a theory. It is expressed in many age-old saying like 'do unto others', or 'what goes around' or 'judge not lest—' well, you know.

This foundational principle that many indigenous cultures have that we are all connected to each other and to the earth is manifested in the external reality of things like slave uprisings, mutiny, junta's, coup de ta's, company walk-outs, strikes, and the general concept of anarchy. People cannot take too much suffering. Any harm done to others will wind up causing harm to those inflicting the harm. Because the reality is that neither animals nor humans do well in unhealthy circumstances, and there will always eventually be an uprising. Unfortunately, this is usually after great damage has been done, and those who have suffered have run out of tolerance. Narcissists inevitably create unhealthy circumstances for those around them because they do not think in terms of the collective. They think in terms of ME, ME, ME. That ME will purchase a boat that looks all shiny and new to impress people, but it is probably made with cheap materials and in a shoddy manner because the narcissist didn't pay the craftsmen and women what they were worth, didn't give them any kind of healthcare, and over-worked them so they could get the boat built as quickly as possible and thus those workers weren't able to do the best job they could do.

Ok enough of the boat metaphor. The bottom line is that narcissists constantly make decisions that eventually lead to their downfall. And though it may take a while, and they may actually rise very high (Richard Nixon/Bill Cosby/Harvey Weinstein), the harder they come, the harder they fall.

It is so sad to me, that despite the fact that history has shown us time and again that corrupt empires always eventually fail, those who achieve great power over others continue to exploit those others for their own benefit. One of the main reasons that this happens I assume, is that it does appear that exploiting other people works—and quite well. Cruelty, exploitation, and self-interest seems to garner people a great deal of success and even respect. This success and respect can last a very long time and produce powerful results.

America has been one of the most powerful nations in history, and it was built on slavery and genocide. Our model was Europe, and prior to the colonization of that land by the Romans, the slave-trade had already reached back pretty far into history, however different it may have been. I often wonder if one of those differences might have been the use of rape … Greco-Roman culture is known historically to have used violence and rape as a form of control over the many people they conquered—the term 'pederasty,' which was a sexual relationship between an older man and a young boy, was socially acceptable during Greek and Roman rule[5].

The Roman empire lasted for over 2000 years and created the culture and country of Europe which became the most powerful nation on earth having now colonized, well, almost everybody at some point. I mean, we do all speak English, French, or Spanish! European colonized countries and continents include Australia, Africa, South America, North America (Canada), Central America, Hong Kong, South Asia, and the Middle East; minus North China and Japan, that is pretty much the whole world. This cultural legacy of Europe has been spread around the globe, and based on recorded Greco-

Roman history and the testimony of many indigenous people, it has involved massive amounts of slavery, oppression, abuse, rape, pedophilia, and narcissism. I don't know as much about this legacy for other cultures, but I know it is true for ours. Movies like *The Joy Luck Club* (1993), *Bandit Queen* (1995), and *Desert Flower* (2009) show a history of brutality that has existed in all cultures, but I can only speak effectively on my own personal experience, and the U.S. was indeed founded by slavers, racists, pedophiles, and narcissists. I am aware though, that every other country that was colonized by Europe has the narrative of slavery, racism, pedophilia, and narcissism.

Those narcissists are on our money, statues of them are in our parks, schools, and hospitals, and government buildings are named after these slavers, racists, pedophiles, and narcissists. You know, like DeSoto, Columbus, Lee, Washington, Jefferson, Jackson …

It is only now that I am noticing just how many movies have Harvey Weinstein's name in the credits. A lot of narcissists are able to procure and maintain power using coercion, violence, rape, manipulation, and subversive tactics. As stated, they are often violent, always abusive, pathological liars, and they create chaos in their personal lives and the lives of the people around them.

The movie I mentioned earlier, *Mommie Dearest* (1981) had a HUGE impact on me the first time I saw it as a child. I felt like Christina! For those of you who haven't seen it, Christina was the abused daughter of narcissistic actress Joan Crawford. I was astounded to see that someone else was having a similar experience to mine. What really affected me was how the daughter portrayed that her mother would become enraged over the strangest things like using the wrong hangers, not finishing food, and learning to swim.

It was the same for me. Leaving an un-wiped spot on the kitchen counter, having candy wrappers in my backpack, forgetting to close a door—these things would cause my mother to fly into a rage. It made absolutely no logical sense. It caused me to carry around consistent feelings of anxiety, worry, and fear. I never quite knew what to expect. She would wake me up at 2 am on a school night to wipe a spot I missed on the counter (in the 5th grade). If I didn't keep my room spotless, I would be restricted from going outside. If I got anything less than all A's—the same.

Honestly, regarding most of it, I don't even really remember why I was hit, punished, or on restriction most of my childhood. I was just always in my room, by myself, crying. I expended a great deal of energy trying to make sure everything was always perfect to avoid stress, but it never worked. There was always something wrong. My home (all of them) was always charged with some kind of intense negative emotion. Whether it was between my mother and my stepfather, or just my mother, there was never any peace.

In addition to the stressful environment my mother maintained, my sister's father was always angry, and he expressed that anger freely. He would kick in doors, kick holes in the walls, and beat on all three of us. I watched him break my mother's jaw once, and he beat me often. The other piece of it that took me years to process, is that thing I mentioned where he would make me strip naked when he spanked me, which is of course really effing sick for a grown man to do to a small girl. I am so thankful it never went farther than that, but he was consistently inappropriate. He would walk around the house 'bucket-necked' as they say, all the time. It made me so uncomfortable. Probably the worst thing he ever did, was force me to let him cut all my hair off when I was about 9 years old. It was so traumatic. I remember sitting on that stool just crying my eyes out as I watched my hair fall to the ground in clumps.

By the time I left home, my nerves were shot, SHOT I tell you! This anxiety and fear stayed with me for the next 25 years after leaving my mother's house, and that affected so much of my life in harmful ways. In other words, long after the stress that I could not control ended, I continued to manufacture stressful situations in my own life. I had developed an eating disorder, had a good case of OCD, did quite a lot of drinking and drugs in college, and suffered from frequent suicidal thoughts and depression.

Now that I've seen so many accounts of child abuse, I realize that my experience wasn't even close to how bad it can be. So many people have suffered way worse than I did, with sexual abuse, torture, and straight-up maniacal circumstances like being raised in a cult or held hostage for years.

What I noticed though, is that their stories contain many of the same elements as mine, especially in terms of describing the personality of the person who abused them. And unfortunately, the outcome for these victims has also been the same. I've noticed that many people who were raised by narcissists are very cynical, feel a great deal of self-doubt, and are constantly explaining themselves.

I heard a psychiatrist say that living with a narcissist is a full-time job. The long-term effects though, are to me the most difficult part of being raised by or being in a relationship with a narcissist. The trauma creates cycles that continue long past your experience with them, and it is so incredibly difficult to identify and eradicate those cycles. The truth is that the mind desperately needs to heal, and so it will continue to regenerate certain experiences until the healing occurs. I call this The Loop.

The Loop

When I was studying for my Master's in Psychology, one of the most fascinating experiments that I read about was in *The Behavior of Organisms* (Skinner, 1938) on conditioning using lab rats. The experiment was an amazing metaphor for what it was like to be raised by a narcissist. Among his many experiments was one with three controls; one was a rat that was given food pellets from a dispensary for a short period of time, and then no food pellets were dispensed ever again; that rat came back to the dispensary for a little while looking for pellets, but eventually gave up when they never came; the second control was a rat who was consistently given food pellets, it never ceased, and that rat consistently came to the dispensary for the food pellets; the third and final control was a rat who was given food pellets from the dispensary off and on; sometimes the rat would come to the dispensary for a food pellet and was given one, and sometimes no food pellets came out, but that rat never stopped going back to the dispensary hoping and waiting for a food pellet to come out[6]. Skinner remarked in a section labeled 'Periodic Reconditioning' that "If the reconditioning is periodically repeated ... the strength of the reflex remains at a constant value, so long as the periodic reconditioning is maintained[7]."

This is how narcissists control everyone around them. It's called intermittent conditioning. They identify what you want and/or need, and they give it to you every now and then, or in the case of a romantic relationship, they give it to you a whole lot at the beginning of the relationship, and you spend the rest of the relationship trying to get it back.

Imagine how much more detrimental this is to a child who does not a have a choice to 'get out' of the relationship, so must navigate these unpredictable waters of the narcissistic parent's constantly changing emotions. Narcissists will basically behave in whatever way they think will get them the most immediate results which is often yelling, criticizing, or violence, but they will also be nice (usually by providing material things or assistance). They will do whatever will manipulate the situation faster. They will sometimes capitulate, be charming, and give you gifts every now and then. You get caught in a loop of adapting to the emergencies, hoping for the warm-fuzzies, and riding out the disappointment of never being able to maintain a consistent atmosphere of love. It becomes like a dance to which your body and brain adjust their settings, and since you never quite figure out exactly which combination of moves will prevent a breakdown, you are pretty much walking around in a constant state of anxiety. After 18 years, it is very familiar, and you have become an expert at existing in that framework.

By the time you are an adult, you know how to manage a narcissist. Obviously, most of us have no idea this is what we are doing, and as mentioned before if you are in any way observant of the world's stage, what you are dealing with seems pretty normal. In the context of domestic and child abuse, sex-trafficking, murder, mass shootings, political corruption, corporate corruption, addiction, illness, war and all of the suffering that seems to be running rampant in the world right now, how big a deal is one person in your life who is very controlling, mean, and dishonest? Surely one can deal with that.

This is especially true for marginalized communities. It is too easy to continue operating in the detrimental cycles created in the environment of a mentally ill person once you get out into the world because the sad fact is that much of the world is operating in the same way.

At this point, I believe that many of the people who have power over us are probably mentally ill considering the new information we are beginning to identify regarding mental illness. As John Lennon said, "Our society is run by insane people." So, you leave a house with someone who is slowly destroying themselves and everyone around them, and you go out into a world that is slowly being destroyed by the people who run it. How in the world is it possible to operate in a healthy manner?

Now what really compounds this quandary of human behavior is the stability of the nature of its expression, meaning, how stuck everyone can get in this loop. Children MUST bond with their caretaker; it is the only way for them to get their needs met. There must be some level of prioritizing another's person's needs for a parent to take care of their children. This is almost impossible for a narcissist, or at least only in spurts for the camera or to achieve their own objective.

For narcissists, children are simply an extension of themselves—another piece of their legacy. They expect that child to reflect everything that they want their life to look like, and this may not always encompass the child's needs. If a narcissist values beauty, you will always have to dress nice and behave perfectly. If a narcissist values knowledge, you will have to get good grades and be smart. If a narcissist values physical prowess, they will probably expect you to be good at sports. What you are interested in won't matter so much. Essentially, you really cannot completely be yourself with a narcissist because it is inevitable that in relationships, sometimes people's needs clash, and they may have to look to other sources to fulfill them.

For a child, in this individualistic climate in America, there aren't too many 'others' to turn to. We are a country of single parents and broken families. So that child must bend their needs to the parent. A child who bonds with someone who does not always take care of their needs is learning that love means a certain amount of neglect—not being nurtured or taken into consideration. In fact, what a child learns is that THEY must take care of the other person's needs in order to get even their basic needs met like food and sleep. What this is beginning to get us dear readers, is a world full of people who never got what they needed as a child to develop into a fully functional human being. And they seem to be everywhere ...

Chapter 3

THE NARCISSISM EPIDEMIC

"You like me, you really like me!" - (Sally Fields accepting her Oscar in1985)

Introduction

I do not think Sally Fields is a narcissist, in fact she seems quite sweet and genuine; her iconic statement is a pure expression of the sentiment we all have that is so often denied to us, which I believe has led to a narcissism epidemic. A child who feels unloved will grow up to become obsessed with getting love, and I believe we have a world full of people who feel unloved. First though, let's take a deeper look into the origins of the word narcissism.

The Greek myth on Narcissus originates from before the birth of Jesus, so this idea that people suffer from mental, emotional, and psychological pathologies is definitely not new. There is an abundance of symbolism and mythology from long ago in cultures all around the world about circumstances that cause people to go 'mad' or lose touch with reality. These thousands of tales of monsters, demons, tricksters, liars, and various power-hungry characters that wreak havoc upon everyone they come into contact with are evidence that as a human race, we have been dealing with destructive beings for a very long time. There has been no shortage of difficult circumstances created by 'evil' forces for humankind to battle from werewolves, to vampires, to zombies. These stories go into fantastic mythic detail about how the monster was created, and this always seems to involve some kind of horrible suffering the monster had to endure that ultimately changed them permanently.

Examples include the man who gets bit by a wolf or the killer who was neglected and abused as a child. I have always noticed varying levels of empathy that people do or do not have for digesting the reasons why someone commits such heinous acts, but the bottom line is there are always reasons. I have noticed that the word 'excuse' seems to be juxtaposed with reasons, and they really don't mean the same thing. Excuse implies an inherent weakness, but reason absolutely confirms it; the critical variable here is an implied lack of self-control. We don't say that someone is using the excuse that they are cold to go back home and get a jacket—they are just cold! The same is true with mental illness. If your brain is damaged, you are not capable of making sound decisions. I think the real problem lies in a cultural tendency towards minimizing suffering, and sometimes just being completely unaware of it. We are not always privy to as much of the gory details in each other's lives when investigating why a person becomes who they are. Documentaries continue to be made about Ted Bundy and Jeffrey Dahmer in an attempt to figure out, well basically WTF? I truly believe though that there has always been something (or numerous things) that happened to people with serious pathologies; some horrible circumstance that would help us understand why they have become what they have become. In Ted Bundy's case there are theories about his abusive father and incest, and with Jeffrey Dahmer there is certainly some attribution to all the psycho-active pharmaceuticals his mother took while she was pregnant.

Our (former) POTUS has a biography rife with circumstances that could easily create a narcissist (a cold calculating father, distant mother, and witnessing the destruction of his brother by his father[1]). There is usually a suggestion of abuse or neglect in the early development of monstrous people, and the vicious cycle this perpetrates of producing generation after generation of dysfunction.

There is always a reason for physical ailments, so it seems logical that there is always a reason for psychological ailments, beyond just being plain old crazy. Perhaps one of the reasons we are beginning to be much more detailed in say, our understanding of serial killers, is because we are producing more and more of these extremely destructive personalities, so we have a lot at stake in terms of keeping our society safe. I don't know for sure if we are now more protected against serial killers, but it does not feel that we are protected at all from narcissists. They seem to be running the planet at this point. And quite brutally in fact.

The one common variable in the wake of brutal acts is the victims of these acts. Century after century has seen massive numbers of people who become casualties of humankind's most heinous stories including war, famine, slavery, genocide, torture, and servitude. Those who have survived such horrors carry the scars of memory and the emotional trauma that suffering creates, and as it is said, one either bends or breaks.

I would say that as the long-term trauma from all this suffering and pain piles up over the march of time, we become more and more damaged as a whole since so many of us fall prey to the brutality of violence and abuse on an individual basis, and truly break under the weight of it all. This means more people are damaged, dysfunctional, and/or depleted from enduring less than ideal to downright highly challenging circumstances that have spread around the entire globe and become more common such as poverty, pollution, war, and various forms of oppression.

This oppression logically trickles down from the peak to the crevasses of society. What you put into something is what you get out, and this applies to pretty much everything in life. If you use the right ingredients, cook at the right temperature for the right amount of time, you will wind up with a beautiful dish that is delicious. In the same way, the proof of a well-balanced society is in the state of the people that occupy that society.

Some History

"Great name. Nunavik. Love it. Uh, sorry for stealing all the land. Anyway, we got a hockey game we're watching so …" - (Jim Gaffigan on Canada) Pale Tourist (2020)

There is no doubt in my mind that every society has had to deal with mental illness and those unable to function fully as a result, so it is tricky trying to really pinpoint a cause. This is because every culture has experienced circumstances and conditions that cause intense human suffering that can lead to mental illness. There are various ways that those with problems handling over-whelming suffering (which is what mental illness is) cope with their illness. This can range from addiction to some form of disassociation, but places for them to reside have certainly been a necessity since functioning in society for them is often challenging or even impossible. Since the U.S. is a nation begun and built by the British after ousting the French and Spanish colonizers, the history of Britain's treatment of the mentally ill seems most relevant in our attempt at unraveling this epidemic.

The fact that Europe and many of its colonies through-out the globe have a large number of what we used to call Insane Asylums, but now refer to as Psychiatric Hospitals, is also pretty noteworthy. There is a history now that dates back a few hundred years, originating from around the world and Europe, of institutions built for those human beings that cannot function autonomously for reasons of physical or mental handicaps. We have not always been as responsible for those with handicaps according to our recent recorded history, in fact even condemning people who were born with or developed some type of debilitating illness, to various states of terrible conditions of confinement, and regarding them in terms such as 'feeble-minded' or 'mad.' In my research, it seems clear that how responsible a community or government is for the care of the mentally ill, and how many of those poor souls have to be provided for is directly related to the health of that society.

European Monasteries and Hospitals were the initial care-takers of the insane, but this responsibility eventually shifted to small private facilities which began to proliferate in the 1600's. Over time facilities grew from numerous small private domiciles, to larger institutions in order to deal with the growing number of people suffering from mental illness. In the 18th century in Britain, there were an estimated 17 of these 'private madhouses' with less than 30 patients, but about seven larger institutions outside of London with more[2]. By the end of the 19th century, Britain and France combined had a few hundred patients in asylums, and by the turn of the century, hundreds of thousands. The U.S. topped this number by an increase of 927% in asylum patients by the mid 20th century[3]. From general neglect and abuse such as chaining patients to beds and poorly ventilated rooms, to shock therapy and lobotomies, as well as the extermination of thousands of mentally ill patients by the Nazi's, I would not say we have a pleasant history in our treatment of the mentally ill. Thanks in part to the diagnosis of George III with mental illness[4] (who btw during his rule saw 1.6 million Africans transported into slavery[5]), there was a brief period in the 1700's during Europe's 'Age of Enlightenment' when the populous began its 'dismantling of religious and monarch authority', where there were some compassionate reforms to the treatment of the mentally ill by various ethical physicians[6]. However, the rapidly elevating numbers of patients quickly aborted this era. Over-crowding and no funding during wartime once again led to notorious abuse of patients in asylums including starvation, physical abuse, neglect, and poor hygienic and general living conditions[7]. In the U.S., there were over 250 mental institutions built in the 1800's[8]. There are now 692 actual Psychiatric Hospitals, but there are 4,665 outpatient facilities as of 2018[9]. By the mid 20th century in the U.S., psychiatric drugs had become the standard method of treatment for the mentally ill, but the number of patients steadily rose and continues to this day[10].

There is now a modern narrative carved into our collective psyche about the evil of Insane Asylums in probably over a hundred horror movies such as *Halloween II* (2009), *Gothika* (2003), *Hellbound: Hellraiser II* (1988), *Shutter Island* (2010), *Stonehearst Asylum* (2014), *House on Haunted Hill* (1999), and the infamous *One Flew Over the Cuckoo's Nest* (1975). The tricky part has been determining what it actually means to be considered mad, crazy, feeble-minded, cuckoo—all the words for mentally ill. What does it take now to get that label or diagnosis? And the real question relevant to this work is, does it always mean one cannot function? Are there some shades of grey between healthy and institutionalized? I suggest the answer is a resounding YES.

Our acceptance of insanity as an actual illness to be treated rather than a handicap to be managed has opened the door to deeper understanding of what mental illness really is. This has allowed us to study it and the people affected by it with reduced bias. Probably one of the most glaring discoveries has revealed itself through the study of serial killers and the realization that most of them operate like normal (even exceptional to some degree) citizens. This subject has made it abundantly clear that crazy isn't always shown by exaggerated dysfunction, but that it can also lurk quite secretly and quietly below the surface of an apparently normal human being. I think we can all agree that it is probably easier to understand how a child who grows up in poverty, around violence, and/or addiction can evolve into a violent person themselves, but it is a little harder to understand how someone like Hitler or slave-owners came to be.

Europe and America certainly aren't the only cultures guilty of creating conditions that appear to have nurtured the proliferation of mental illness and psychological pathologies. The reality though, is that we have been the leaders of a new world for the past few centuries thanks to global European colonialization and subsequent economic dominance, so it seems the most relevant to study that culture regarding what seems to be a growing mental illness epidemic. My assertion that there is a narcissism epidemic is based on the fact that there is a mental illness epidemic, and this can at least be suggested by the rampant use of anti-depressants, anti-psychotics and anti-anxiety drugs, school shootings, the over-prescription of Ritalin to children, and the millions of diagnoses of ADD, OCD, and borderline personalities[11].

There have been constant mass shootings for the last two decades, and the proliferation of mental illness diagnoses has become a part of the fabric of our society. College students now take drugs that were once only prescribed for illness, just to stay up to study for exams. The average person takes drugs that were once available only to the very wealthy or for very serious pain. Children now take drugs that only adults used to take—and it is the very young that are mainly over-dosing on opioids[12].

The cherry-on-top is that we (had) a bona-fide narcissist as the POTUS. To put it plainly, the recent President of the so-called Free World has a mental illness. This to me is the ultimate symbol of narcissism having become a cultural trait. What I am suggesting basically, is that narcissism is one of the most common, and probably undiagnosed mental illnesses in America today, and I want to explore why, how, and who is being affected by it.

My questions are: What are the underlying reasons in our present society for this epidemic? Why do there seem to be so many narcissists around these days? From the White House to your house, I am hearing a LOT of people say they have a narcissist in their life.

Why

Is there something different about our culture and our society; some variance from other cultures that could be contributing to an epidemic of narcissism? We are all aware of the narrative about America being the 'land of the free' and the place everyone wants to come to for the opportunity to build a better life. Why life here is 'better' than the places immigrants are coming from is a whole other book on the history of colonization and what the corporations that were set up because of the sugar, tea, coffee, palm oil, diamonds, metals, rubber, silver and gold that is abundant in these colonized resource-rich countries (Africa/Australia/South America/North America/Asia) created in terms of long-term effects. That was a long sentence, but it basically means we became rich from stealing resources from other countries. Those books have already been written by the way … I would say however, that a narcissism epidemic is one of those long-term effects! Other effects include poverty, addiction, environmental damage, economic slavery, scarcity, and ethnic division based on who was favored for labor and servitude. All of these lines and borders that were drawn through these resource-rich continents now delineate areas of great suffering for the people left behind in the wake of the war and violence created by the businesses that set up shop there. For the sake of limiting our focus however, let's just look at some basic cultural differences.

There is one very big difference between Eastern and Western as well as ancient and modern cultures that can account for irregularities in terms of how our societies have evolved. This difference is collectivist versus individualist.

The Eastern and more ancient cultures (meaning having established powerful empires over two-thousand years ago like China), had what we refer to as collectivist cultures, and the Western and more modern countries like Europe and North America have what we refer to as individualistic cultures[13]. The basic difference is that collectivists prioritize the collective, or the group, and individualists prioritize the individual. Collectivists are always going to make choices that appear to be good for the whole, and individualists will make choices that appear to be good for each person.

The idea that I find compelling here, is that the extreme of either approach can be very destructive for human beings. The extreme of collectivism, or a culture that prioritizes the functioning of the whole, is the sacrifice of the individual. This practice has been expressed in various ways in some of those more ancient cultures with things like ritualistic human sacrifice, servitude, or rigid systems of role expectations based on biological or inherited factors that may not apply to every person that falls into those categories. For example, the traditional expectations that women should focus on taking care of the home will be difficult for women who are more ambitious or athletic, and the expectation that a man should willingly sacrifice his life in a war will be difficult for men who are more artistic or domestic.

Perhaps as a response to this, we have developed over time into a more individualistic society, taking into account the diversity of human make-up. I have always thought that the more ancient societies made a huge mistake in over-looking the pain caused to the minority who were sacrificed to serve the well-being of the many, and that it was inevitable that this minority would begin to buck the system.

I mean, who wants to be thrown into the volcano? Even though it may be one person out of a thousand once a year, it really sucks for that one person's loved ones. So as the number of those aggrieved individuals grew over time, maybe people began to become more socialized to more individualistic behavior. Now however, we are reaching an extreme with regards to this personal freedom. This is not to say that absolutely every culture in our human history had these extreme imbalances, but many of them did. It also makes sense to me that those people would probably be the most violent due to their imbalances and thus conquer everyone else, because when you are balanced, you are peaceful. Peaceful people don't want to take over the world.

The extreme of individualism is prioritizing the self, and whatever one identifies with that self over everything else. The individual has now become extremely pre-occupied with freedom of choice, to the point of complete avoidance of anything that causes personal discomfort, and the utter devaluation of taking other's concerns into account. It's cool to not be thrown in the volcano, but now everybody wants to be rich and famous. This level of self-identification has grown to huge proportions due to the rewards associated with focusing on the self such as fame, success, and victory, and I believe it has now morphed into an epidemic of narcissism.

Narcissism used to be a term associated with a few extreme icons like Caligula or King Henry VIII who possessed such a grandiose concept of identity that it manifested into destructive, selfish acts reminiscent of those with personality disorders like psychopathy or sociopathy. Narcissism has traditionally been a description of your garden variety of arrogance and self-centeredness, but it has now become such a celebrated and prevalent personality type, that our country elected a clinical narcissist as our leader. That he is so supported and loved by such a large segment of the population, and that we are seeing such a rise in heinous acts and a resurgence (at least publicly) of severe racism and intolerance, is proof that we have reached a level of individualism that has become very dangerous. Considering the fact that this narcissistic POTUS and many other dictatorial-like leaders seem to be popping up globally (Putin/Kim Jong Un/Bulsonaro/Duterte/ISIS), it may even be dangerous to the very survival of our planet.

This individualism-turned-narcissism is celebrated in our popular culture and has been revealed to be a disturbing trend that has existed under-ground for some time (possibly since World War II and the Nazi sentiment), but it is now quite boldly out in the light of day, in all its destructive, violent, intolerant, self-serving glory.

Let's face it, narcissists are very attractive to people. Sexy even. A woman married Ted Bundy in jail! Cardi B. admitted to robbing and possibly raping men, but we love her okurrrrrr! They have a lot of character traits that Americans are particularly excited by: confidence (at least on the outside), swagger, style, bluster, bravado, gift of gab, beauty, and some level of skill or prowess. They love attention, so they go out of their way to do things to

KEEP our attention. People voted for Trump because he is their superhero. We are very prone to not only letting them in our life but giving them a great amount of influence over it and us as well. We trust that they are the expert or the great friend or lover that they appear to be, unaware for a while that they are actually sucking us dry, slowly, over time.

Why do we love these people? Why is this such a celebrated personality type? How did America come to value this type of personality? When you look at other cultural stereotypes, like the shadowy Russian, the hyper-serious Asian, the stoic Native, or the celebratory African, you can see that certain cultures value certain traits such as bravery and courage, intelligence and wisdom, or inclusiveness and joy. You cannot deny that in America, we like the super-stars. Our icons are people who deeply expressed their individuality like Michael Jackson, Elvis Presley, and Marilyn Monroe. They were all highly creative, had a unique style, and were considered quite attractive. Interesting innit that all three are dead …. from drug overdose …

Probably one of the clearest answers to why the narcissistic personality became such an American staple is Hollywood. America is the birthplace of entertainment and movies. Something about being in such a diverse society somehow created a hot-bed of entertainment. I know we have a powerful military, but forreal, Hollywood is what put America on the global map. Everyone loves our celebrities because film is a medium that crosses oceans. It made being famous possible without being a King or Queen, a writer, or a military leader. Suddenly, what you could do became just as lucrative as what you could get through force. Now you can become as rich as the oil tycoons from acting and singing or posting pictures of your cat on Instagram.

And hey, don't get me wrong, I friggin LOVE cute animals, I just wish teachers were paid as much as people with cute cats. This is a brand-new phenomenon that truly has its roots in the Western world. Hollywood has affected the entire globe, but I would suggest it has been a perfect breeding ground for narcissism because of the massive amounts of money that have been made, and the fact that the foundation of that money was made from slavery and the genocide of the Indigenous people of this land. Extremely large amounts of money were made by the European conquerors of and settlers in this land from cotton, so America has truly profited from a dirty industry and very brutal beginnings. Cotton, gold, oil, steel, fast food, cosmetics, pharmaceuticals, technology; this is a very wealthy nation as a result of all that slavery and genocide.

Who

"Poets, Priests and Politicians, have words to thank for their position, words that scream for your submission." – The Police, Dedododo, Dedadada (1980)

Now it's important to note again that there have always been narcissists. I am not suggesting that narcissism was born in the U.S., but to suggest it's an epidemic now means that there were only a few recognizable ones, and now they are everywhere. What is the difference between who it used to be, who it is now, and why the numbers seem to be increasing?

We used to view narcissists as people who really stood out, and really, the word narcissist has not actually been used to refer to many people that we now know fell under that category to some extent. For the past few decades, we have used the terms psychopath and sociopath more and more instead of criminal or insane in our recognizing that there are some very dangerous people in our society. The word narcissist has been used to describe people who we considered extremely self-centered, so the addition of narcissism as an actual personality disorder, or NPD, as listed in the DSM-5, clearly ups-the-anti on exactly how serious it is to recognize that someone is a narcissist.

I suggest that the foundation for psychopathic, sociopathic, or any of the other anti-social personality types that were present in people like John Wayne Gacy and Ed Gein, involves—no—REQUIRES, narcissism. This is whether they are one themselves, or the victim of one.

Like I said, there is almost always some horrific child-hood story associated with tyrants, psychopaths, and sociopaths that explains how they may have become such a destructive person. When there isn't, I truly believe it's just because we don't know it. People go to their graves with lots of secrets. The reality is that one only needs to look at some of the world's oldest documents like the Bible or the Koran to see that there have always been ruthless and violent people with great power. King David sent a dude to his death so he could have his wife—and it wasn't even some great powerful love, just physical attraction. Over a long human history, royalty, military leaders, pirates (a.k.a. colonizers, a.k.a. explorers), priests and shamans, slavers, politicians, lawyers, doctors, police, business tycoons, C.E.O.'s, the rich in general, and anybody in charge have shown us the possibilities for oppression of those who are vulnerable. Some people do good things with their power, like Princess Di or Oprah Winfrey, and some people do really bad things with it, like Jim Jones or Jeffrey Epstein. They have the privilege to achieve it, and the pathology to motivate it.

Interestingly enough, this is a concept that seems to go along with what it takes to even get into a position of power. Specialized circumstances combined with intense sacrifices defines the process of becoming a marine, a doctor, a lawyer, or a priest—you know, no pain, no gain. The level of suffering one must endure to get into a position of power is something that those who achieve it have often already experienced, thus they are easily able to deal with it. They have probably actually developed an intricate way of operating that assists greatly with enduring suffering. I don't believe it's a coincidence that there have been so many entertainers who eventually disclose sexual abuse in their childhood.

To put it simply, suffering requires that you become tough. It's easier to be successful in such a demanding business when you are tough. It is when you become the same type of brutal person that you endured that differentiates us. Tough is valuable; being able to weather storms, endure difficult circumstances with patience, or hold up under life pressures with dignity and grace is a powerful thing and very handy for longevity. It is tricky though, balancing that line between tough and brutal. Perhaps another pre-determination for who has tendencies towards narcissism, is the level of comfort they possess with and for brutality.

In general, I am suggesting that an atmosphere of slavery and genocide would certainly tip the scales on how many people are conditioned into tolerating brutality. It would certainly lay the foundation for what is valued in a society, and how you get power in that society.

And listen, one of the things the narcissists in your life are always trying to trick you into thinking about yourself is that you are weak because you are unable to stand their brutality. "You're so sensitive." "You take things too personally." "You're so dramatic." "You need a thicker skin." These are the things that narcissists say to you.

Unfortunately, sometimes these things may have some truth to them. Like I said earlier, one of the very strategic things that narcissists do is tell a little bit of the truth, and that mixed with lies can throw you off and make it difficult to see how much they lie. The question always is then, is this true? Are you too sensitive? Should you be able to handle someone being cruel to you without it hurting you and causing you to react? I mean, it certainly helps in life to have some level of detachment to cruelty in a world where there is so much of it, because you are able to continue functioning and can therefore gather more resources to get to a place where you are not as much at the mercy of outside forces. But maybe another really relevant question when dealing with narcissists is, even if this is true about me, is it really so deep that I should feel horrible about myself?

I will say this: one truth is that societies that have developed a high level of acceptance for brutality create a history and an atmosphere that allows for a smoother transition into the proliferation of slavery, oppression, abuse, and narcissism.

Slavery & Genocide

"We've made a legend out of a massacre." - James Baldwin, I Am Not Your Negro (2016)

Let us be very clear and honest: the U.S. is a land that was originally inhabited by a large group of people indigenous to this land. They had been here for 10's of thousands of years, had a very distinct culture and history, and about 400 years ago in 1619, pirates from England hijacked a Spanish ship, stole the Africans that were on that ship for the purpose of enslavement, and landed off the coast of Virginia[14].

I bet you didn't learn about the stealing slaves part in the Jamestown lesson in High School ... anyway, Europeans began moving to this continent in larger and larger groups because Europe had become too dangerous for them due to religious persecution. The Protestants, Catholics, and Puritans were violently battling each other over how life should be lived based on God's rules. After enough of them had re-located here, they made the decision to forcibly remove the indigenous people from this land, and by remove I mean kill, and make a living on this land from the business of slavery. The fact that they had guns and the current inhabitants did not was a huge help.

Now, prior to that English arrival, in the 1500's the Spanish and the Portuguese had also invaded this land and were slavers as well, so the people who killed the largest amount of the indigenous people, the names of whom were Taino, Choctaw, and Muscogee to name a few, were conquistadors like DeSoto, Ponce de Leon, and Cortez—you know all those street names we have in every town in America.

Just on a sidenote, I have always been astounded at how we have been speaking the names of these deceased Indigenous people all of our entire lives when saying "I am going to" or "are from" Iowa, Tennessee, Milwaukee, North or South Dakota, Idaho, Utah, Alabama, or Mississippi. These are the names of Indigenous American people and landmarks. It is pretty gangster to take people's land, kill them, and then name it after them.

Again, I am not suggesting that no other empire cultivated slavery and genocide. Genghis Khan was considered 'ruler of the world' having conquered most of the continent of Asia in the 13th century. The fact that Europe and the U.S. are now the greatest among these conquerors is really just testament to how much human beings have been engaging in war, slavery, and conquering one another for a very long time. The Romans did it for about 3000 years having conquered the Greeks, parts of North and East Africa, the Middle East, and what we now call Europe, and they achieved this by inflicting massive amounts of violence, rape, and torture on the inhabitants of these lands. If you think about it, our parent country (Europe) was forged from the ruins of war … could explain that culture … maybe group PTSD? Just a thought …

Dating from before Roman conquest, the Arabs had been invading the Middle East, parts of Asia, Mediterranean Europe, and North and East Africa for almost a thousand years, Russia had conquered most of Asia by the 17th century, and from Alexander the Great, to Julius Caesar, to Charlemagne, the people in the empires of the Eastern hemisphere (Asia, Africa, Europe) had experienced some level of violent conflict and war since, well for a long freakin time as it appears in our historical documents. Centuries. Millennia. This is relevant to the possibility for such a heinous act like the conquering of an entire continent to have occurred, because the fact that it was possible, carried out by enough people to create an empire out of it, and subsequently supported by the people in those empires, means that there has been a collective acceptance of brutality, slavery, and violence as a means of gaining power for quite a while.

I believe though, that looking at our own recent and collective participation in this particular chapter of human violence is relevant to understanding how we have gotten to where we are now in the U.S., because it is just easier to make connections to more recent history. We also have a very unique, modern culture that was forged in distinct circumstances with their own specific qualities that have led to a very unique outcome—which is rampant narcissism.

There have definitely been other extremely negative long-term consequences of being conquered through-out our global history, but I think never before have we seen it have such a pervasive, multi-dimensional, and destructive effect as we are seeing now in our recorded history, facing as it were, the possible destruction of human life on our planet. Watching all that wildlife begin to burst through the cracks of the abandoned city of Chernobyl truly brings the point home that the Earth could indeed survive something that would destroy human beings.

And what happened to all those empires? What happened to Egypt? To Rome? To Persia? To Mongolia? To Russia? They are gone. Dead and gone. They all came to an eventual bloody downfall when the people who were being crushed under their oppressor's feet could no longer endure the suffering and rose up in violence. But the U.S. is the grandchild of that bloody Roman Empire, and this country has used the same methods of murder, rape, torture, religious persecution, and slavery (along with a huge dose of their latest creation, racism) to acquire many other lands and their aforementioned abundant resources.

So here we are, the great U.S.A., 400 years in on the latest empire gained by force. French, Spanish, and British pirates sailed over in their ships from cultures of great violence and conquest like those of all the European monarchies. Starting in the 1400's, and prior to that 1619 landing in Jamestown, the 15th and 16th centuries of England were ruled by vicious monarchs that led global colonization missions. This included Henry VI, who was diagnosed as insane after being un-responsive for an entire year following a defeat in battle (a diagnosis he may have inherited in part from his maternal grandfather Charles VI of France who was also declared insane in his last years), Richard III as dramatized in the Shakespeare play, Henry VIII who we all know had two of his wives executed, Mary I or "Bloody Mary," Elizabeth I who executed her cousin, a lover, and suffered from severe depression towards the end of her life, and James I—yes the one whose name is on the cover of your Bible, and who was responsible for the death of 100's of women accused of being witches, as well as with conquering all of Scotland and Ireland.

Oh, and James might be yet another true narcissist, based on his declaration that kings had a divine right as being higher than other human beings and could well, basically do what they wanted. It is noteworthy to point out that it is during James I reign that slavery was really systemically solidified in the U.S.

This was a time in Europe's history when the plague was killing people by the thousands (Covid-19 is not our first plague), and there had been constant war. King James' approved version of the Bible had both removed and re-translated much of the original works of that document, and most of the war and conflict going on at that time was about religion. And this great promoter of Christianity—he was most likely bi-sexual. There are several notable documentations of letters between he and his male lovers as proof[15].

King James became an alcoholic and died terribly ill and beset with disease, pretty much like almost every monarch previous. George III was diagnosed with mental illness, as well as Queen Isabella of Spain, and Queen Victoria. Shakespeare dedicated much of his literature to the stories of these people, and these classics of literature are riddled with tales of betrayal, incest, rape, murder, and mental illness.

So perhaps it is safe to say that the narrative of our being 'discovered' by super-hero-like explorers and formed from the ideas of freedom and democracy, is actually a surface rendition of a story that is really about violent, mentally ill psychopaths who had no problems with killing an entire land of people and transporting another group of people to that land as slaves to create a better life for themselves than the one they were escaping—one that had been plagued by viruses, war, rape, and intolerance. Is it any surprise then, that the U.S. was poisoned from its beginnings by racism and intolerance?

I know it is so difficult to peruse these polarizing concepts in this time of such extreme division, but it is much easier to know the best way to go forward, when you are clear on where you have come from. I suppose we can all at least agree that major atrocities in our recent human history would include the Roman conquests, slavery, and Nazi Germany. There is so much footage of all the horrible things that happened during World War II, but not so much from the 400 years of slavery in the Southern U.S. besides pictures and literature. Thanks to Hollywood and especially Netflix, we are just now really beginning to see portrayals of what life as a slave could have been like.

This is so important, because as humans we are very visually oriented, and having images shown over and over creates certain narratives that entire societies will adopt beliefs about, like with the Nazi's. When you can see 500 Jews lined up next to a pit they were forced to dig, and watch mothers with babies in their arms shot to death and fall into this pit and create a sea of dead bodies, it affects you viscerally. We have not been able to see moving pictures of plantation owners raping women, raping men outside in front of their family, cutting women's breasts off, cutting men's penises off and displaying them in jars on the mantle, chopping off limbs, whipping people to death on a weekly basis, hanging people, disemboweling people, sending dogs to tear them apart, tying one leg to one horse, the other leg to another horse, and beating the horses to run in opposite directions so that the person's body is ripped in half, and other such un-imaginable forms of violence. But they did indeed all occur for at least 400 years during the birth of this nation.

Who were the people able to do these things? Who were the men and the women that were descendants of people who had re-located here from another land, that had it in them to own human beings and subject them to the worst atrocities? Who is able to whip, maim, or kill someone at 4 pm, and sit down to dinner with their family at 6 pm? What kind of person is able to whole-heartedly believe that another human being is less valuable than a dog? These are serious questions to ask when discussing the formation of a culture.

Because understand this, LOTS of money was made during these 400 years for the people who participated in these dastardly acts and the European monarchs who funded this conquest. That money has been passed down through generations to create an entire new empire full of banks, corporations, colleges and universities, social institutions, and one of the mightiest military complexes on the globe. If the origin of all the money that the U.S. made is from slavery, that clearly delineates in our culture what it takes to make large amounts of money. Since money is what we all need to survive, it follows to me that we would all do whatever we had to do to get that money. That surely seems to encompass having a certain level of required detachment to brutality. If that is what is required, which certainly seems to be the case, then speaking in purely mathematical terms, we have created a nation with a lot of brutal people.

So enough on the brief history lesson. How exactly are narcissists created?

How

What is the nitty-gritty? What are the nasty details of exactly how narcissists develop into who and what they are? First of all, **narcissism is basically a state of distorted identity**. What is identity anyway? It is who you are, or at least who you think you are, which unfortunately for many of us, is completely based on what our experiences have been in the outside world. What people have said about you, how they treat you, the types of interactions you have had and are having are all things that contribute to your sense of identity. These experiences give you information like I am funny, I am small, I am smart, people like me, people dislike me, I matter. These are some of the conclusions we come to based on how others treat us. How others experience you is very much tied-in to how you are experiencing yourself, and this can vary greatly depending on the type of people you are around every day, and what kind of experiences you are having. If you are being treated kindly, given what you need, and having generally positive interactions, you will more than likely FEEL better on the inside.

Of course everybody has certain needs that have to be fulfilled in order to get that inner good feeling. Every human being has basic needs in order to survive including food, water, medicine, hygiene, care, safety, and social inclusion. These are all essential components in the gumbo of how you are being treated. Are you being fed when you are hungry, given hydration when you are thirsty, treatment for your ailments, provided a healthy sanitary environment to help prevent you from getting sick in the first place, given the opportunities for self-expression, being protected from danger, and having beneficial interactions with others? For a very unfortunate group of us, the answer to some of these questions is NO, and there are often dire consequences for not getting these basic needs met.

This is true for every form of life that exists on our planet. Every living thing requires certain conditions and substances for survival. Plants need sun, fish need water, babies need cuddling. As mentioned before, it is an absolute fact that the babies in a crack ward who were held and cuddled have a higher survival rate[16]. I don't think science can dispute at this point in our research and experimental history that human beings need touch, care, contact, and love, so the key to understanding how someone becomes a narcissist is in looking at all the possibilities for different combinations of fulfilled and unfulfilled needs. Having all of your needs met produces a healthy individual; having very few of those needs met will produce an unhealthy, largely dysfunctional individual; having just some of those needs met produces individuals with varied levels of well-being depending on which needs were met and unmet, resulting in varied levels of functionality and dysfunction.

Let's say someone got the food, water, hygiene, and social inclusion, but not the medicine, care, and safety. There could be some health problems, and perhaps a bit of inner turmoil due to not feeling truly valued. Or if you got the social inclusion, care, and safety, but not always the food, water, or hygiene, there would almost definitely be some physical ailments, but perhaps a stronger mind and more peaceful heart. I am sure the possibilities are as endless as there are human beings.

Regarding the specific outcome of becoming a narcissist, I submit that the main ingredients are also the answer to the question which is: **Narcissism is created by a combination of abuse and privilege**. What falls under those categories (abuse/privilege) is wide and varied and can include so many different circumstances, but the one common factor is that all those circumstances would to some extent be a certain amount of suffering and a certain amount of feeling good. The abuse part could range from witnessing someone's suffering, to enduring your own pain. Examples would include you getting a beating yourself, or as a child of a plantation owner, watching your father whip a slave. Both of these are traumatic to children—being on the receiving end, and just witnessing the violence. For the child witnessing the violence his father inflicts, afterwards they would go to a lavish meal cooked by slaves to have supper with family. So, the abuse is witnessing the atrocities of slavery, and the privilege is the advantages given to you as a result of that abuse and for being a slave owner.

When you are witnessing or experiencing trauma, you are generally in a state of fight, flight, or freeze, all fueled by fear. It is traumatic. In order to survive trauma, we must adjust ourselves to circumstances that are too painful to endure in the natural state that we are in at that moment which is one of grief, fear, pain, and/or rage. You really can't function well in those states, so in order to survive traumatic events or circumstances, to some extent you must contract yourself. You must push down what you are actually feeling so that you can eat, sleep, work, and just get through each day.

Having to do this over and over for years makes this contraction become a habit, and it is usually rewarded by the person who is abusing you, because after all, it allows them to continue to abuse you. If you aren't complaining about or responding to their abuse, why would they stop? If you become comfortable with watching someone be beaten, that would make it easier for the person doling out the beating to continue with it. There is no one to stop them. You are thus slowly conditioned into functioning in a way that is completely in opposition to what you are actually feeling. You are acting. This causes you to develop an identity that is not your true self. This identity is one that tolerates abuse, so it really works best when you are in abusive circumstances. As mentioned earlier, this is why those of us who were abused tend to consistently be pulled to people who will abuse us. It is familiar, we know how to function with that, and we have been rewarded for it over and over—this is the conditioning I spoke of earlier with the lab rat experiments. It's the same process for how you get your pets to stick to certain boundaries that make caring for them easier such as waiting to go outside to pee or poop, or not destroying your furniture. What is habitual eventually becomes completely integrated like anything that you do over and over (sports/martial arts/cooking). Eventually it appears that you have actually become the fake personality you created to survive—PERMANENTLY. This is what narcissism is. The long-term, permanent effects of adjustment to trauma. This is the abuse part.

Remember now, that the fake identity has been created at the expense of what one is genuinely feeling, which as I mentioned above includes grief and rage. These are probably the two most difficult emotions to handle as a child—hell, even as an adult. This is why serial killers behave as they do. They were never able or allowed to process and heal their grief and rage. That grief and rage became integrated into their emotional base, and since it has festered for years, it has amplified in intensity and become impossible for them to control. In my opinion, grief and rage are the foundation of most destructive behavior and are probably the true personality of the narcissist. These two emotions are the motivation for murder, suicide, and every harmful act in between. Until we begin to prioritize, as a society, dealing with these aspects of the human condition, we will continue to create monsters like psychopaths and narcissists.

Ok, so how does the privilege part fit in? It is based on a methodology of abusers, which as I stated earlier is known as intermittent conditioning.

This means, they do really nice things for you or try to make you feel really good from time to time. This keeps you attached to them and more willing to endure the abuse part because I mean, who is just going to stay around and take abuse from someone year after year? There has to be some reason to stay and continue to put up with terrible treatment from someone. This takes us back to the rat experiment and the fact that when you have experienced some pleasure or kindness from someone who starts to abuse you, it takes a long time before you realize that this is the combination of treatment you will always get from this person—abuse and kindness.

Because narcissists are so extreme in their behavior, the kindnesses are often extreme as well. They give you money, gifts, and awesome opportunities. They give you things that no one else will give you, and over time, especially if we are talking about a child, you adjust to this back-and-forth by being grateful for the privileges and ignoring the abuse as much as you are able. In fact, allowing an abuser to continue to abuse you is actually built into the fabric of our culture inside the value of respecting your parents.

Well, Hitler could have been someone's parent! Ted Bundy was in fact someone's parent. Should his daughter respect him? Feeling as if you have no choice but to endure a parent's abuse creates a very disintegrated, contradictory personality type. You are actually harboring a great deal of emotional pain, but you also seem to have quite a few reasons to be grateful and happy. It can be damn confusing … does this person love me or hate me? Aren't all families dysfunctional to some degree? Doesn't everyone have flaws? Isn't it a good thing to be tolerant and compassionate? No one is perfect. This constant vacillation between agony and ecstasy keeps one's cortisol levels too high to maintain well-being.

Cortisol is the substance the body produces during stress to trigger high energy and nurture the fight/flight response, and the production of too much cortisol has been scientifically proven to cause life-long ailments[17]. I would suggest that it not only causes physical ailments, but also contributes to the development of psychological ailments and pathologies. Most pathologies are defined as such because they impair some kind of essential bodily function, which ultimately means organ function. Well, the brain is an organ too!

So back to the privilege—all the gifts and goodies can create a personality that feels they possess inherent access to the good things in life, because it was always the counterbalance to the abuse that was doled out. This is reminiscent of the spoiled rich kid who cannot handle things not going their way. If things going your way was the prize for enduring abuse, you can imagine that the person on the receiving end would become addicted to the 'things going your way' part because the 'abuse' part feels so bad that it would make you compulsive about feeling good, and this my friends is at the foundation of most of the self-destructive things we do.

Everyone just wants to feel good. When you are the victim of constant abuse, regular things don't really feel that great. You need a really BIG feel-good to come up from the horrible down (grief and rage) that abuse makes you feel. That big feel-good is what creates the narcissists. It comes from them enduring terrible abuse, and then being privileged to receive fantastic gifts. This is how their world is structured from a very young age, this is the pattern they live in, and they continue this cycle into their own adulthood. Endure suffering; demand the privilege.

Essentially, narcissists create other narcissists. And yes, I am suggesting that many people who abuse their children are narcissists. It is certainly understandable that interactions with adults can make you want to throttle people sometimes, but children are so innocent when they are small. They cause very few serious problems unless there are special circumstances like a handicap or illness. Anyone who has no problem constantly doling out violence to a child has no ability to truly care for another person's well-being. Violence is the easiest way to control another human being, and I truly believe it often just comes down to what's more convenient for the person in charge, and that the child's welfare is quite secondary.

I have seen this process of narcissists creating other narcissists many times in my own life. I have watched the progression of close cherished friends and relatives through-out their development, and the process of them being slowly turned into a narcissist. The most basic requirement is that you have to have been strongly influenced by a narcissist to become one. It is like a virus. It's catching, as they used to say. It's beyond airborne, it's energyborne, and it seems that more and more people are having a low resistance to this nasty bugger.

We are born innocent, and whatever happens to us in the external world informs our mental, emotional, physical, and psychological development. So, you love the narcissist at first if they are family, and then your relationship just slowly erodes over the years due to constant conflict and hurt. Everyone starts out with a good dose of natural optimism in them to some degree; a basic level of receptivity to love which just feels good to all babies. Kids in healthy environments just want to have fun when young, and they take care of each other. Watching someone you love habitually hurt and injure another person you love is a most painful thing. There's nothing you can really do although heaven knows you try.

Oh the tinder moments I have shared with people who are just no longer in my life ... child-birth, funerals, graduations. It's amazing how you can get to a point with another human being where you definitely can't seem to talk to them without anger bubbling up, but you increasingly just don't even want to be around them because you just know it's going to be painful. The whole interaction will leave you hurting and drained. Everyone is simply not able to endure abuse without having to twist themselves up in some way, force themselves to survive each day and get through it, and make it to the end when you can escape and be free.

I used to watch my mother berate my sister on a daily basis. Nothing was ever good enough. She was always telling or showing her that she was doing something wrong. I remember very clearly that my sister was always crying when she was small. She and I would have so much fun when we were alone, just the two of us. She would hang out with me and my friends even as I became a teen because she was so laid back and peaceful. Once we sat at the corner of Gordon St. and Atwood St. in Atlanta with a lemonade and popcorn stand. She was so cute people bought our stuff even though it was terrible! But over the years as my mother continued to keep both of us in various states of stress as a result of her emotional orientation towards the world and daily life in general, I watched it wear my sister down. She was so sensitive, and so sweet, and so wanting to please, and my mother kept her in a state of constant stress. Unlike me though, she fought back; she was way more fiery. I just took it. It never occurred to me that you could fight your mother back! I was so terrified of her; she used to give me these looks. I swear I thought she wanted to kill me. It hurt me so bad that I would simply shut down and cry. But not my sister. She would fight back.

It was just me and my mother until I was 8 years old, and because she was so emotionally intense, I had already developed an affinity to being alone, because there was nobody else for me to be with. Being alone was much more peaceful. My mother was always on fire. I could never find any comfort with that constant level of daily intense emotion, especially the anger. Oh my God! So many tears, sobbing, crying, yelling, screaming, throwing things, cussing, fighting. Every. Single. Day. Exhausting. I always felt terrible. It was like being sick all the time. Like I said. A virus.

Chapter 4

A VIRUS

(this is how it became an epidemic)

"Exodus 25: The sins of the father are laid upon the children."

Introduction

There is another very compelling side-effect of narcissistic personalities that is a huge contributor to what I see as an epidemic of narcissism. That side-effect is the number of narcissists that are created from one narcissist. They are like viruses that spread through families. The damaging effects from one person who has NPD is vast and wide. They have an amazing impact on the lives of everyone around them. They are able to manipulate and deceive so many of their immediate family, friends, and those in their close environment, and this usually leads to detrimental outcomes for many of those people.

I have always noticed that almost all of the people that closely surround a narcissist are seriously messed-up in some way, and I have also noticed that people close to them and connected to them often get illnesses and even die. Yes, a narcissist will kill you! It is no secret that doctors are making clear connections between disease and stress, and narcissists will keep you in such a constant state of stress, you will almost inevitably become physically or mentally ill.

As we mentioned in the section on the lies, narcissists keep their loved ones in conflict with one another by lying to each of them and telling them different things individually that make them lose trust in one another. They fan any flames of discontent between people, often so they can put themselves in the position of coming in to save the day, or to keep people distracted with drama so they can manipulate behind the scenes to get what they want. They are always surrounded by and involved in stressful situations, and the different ways that people respond and adjust to their abuse creates either immense suffering in individuals who tend to internalize things, or people who become narcissists themselves. They catch the narcissist virus, and as stated by most Psychologists and on *The Sopranos* (1999), there is at present, no cure for narcissism. Thus, catching this virus is deadly.

Contracting the narcissism virus is actually not a highly complex process. Just as bodily fluids can be passed and cause infection, energy can be passed and has measurable effects on a person.

Haven't you ever walked into a room and just felt the vibe from someone's mood? People react in different ways to energy depending on their nature; a comedian may crack a joke to lighten the mood, an empath will want to know what's wrong and help, someone more detached and focused on other things will just want to leave! Unfortunately, upon failure to beat them, many will join them. The propensity for human beings to join in on and copy a group mentality or set of behaviors (like the Nazi's) has been shown in plenty of research, such as the famous Stanford prison experiment from 1971, the results of which were dramatized in the movie *The Stanford Prison Experiment* (2015).

It is said that imitation is the highest form of flattery. It is also a form of connection. Children often automatically copy the behavior of those around them (peekaboo). If you are raised by a narcissist, you will either be very repelled by their behavior and really want to get away from them, or you will mimic their behavior back to them out of a survival mechanism. Often, a little of both will occur. Children have to get their needs met. It is necessary for survival, and a child will bend (endure the abuse until they can get away) or break (do exactly what the narcissist does, like manipulate).

Narcissists are truly uninterested in meeting other people's needs unless it benefits them in some way. The only recourse for someone whose needs are not being met is to lie, use, and steal to get those needs met. So you start pretending, which is a key component to developing a shattered identity. You must pretend to be happy when you are full of rage so that the narcissist won't get pissed off and neglect buying groceries or cooking dinner. You must endure their temper and their petty criticisms to get picked up on time from your extra-curricular activities. You must learn how to be stealth in sneaking around to get the things that you want and need. You must smile and feign happiness when you are with them around other people and they are doing that "aren't I fabulous" act when they may have been screaming at you and berating you for how terrible a person you are just five minutes before. The covert narcissists will brag to people about how wonderful you are though they rail at you in private. You must suppress all your hurt and anger to keep operating on a daily basis when the atmosphere in your house could and does often explode in violence and rage on a weekly or even daily basis. I often felt like I was walking around in a daze while brushing my teeth, bathing, cleaning, doing homework, or just trying to find the joy in living.

Human beings have an un-destroyable need to feel joy for the most part. Even in the middle of the worst circumstances, like slavery or war, we will sing a song, dance, or find something to laugh about. Most of us spend a great deal of our lives pursuing things that give us even a temporary feeling of joy. Narcissists are very tapped-in to this need, and they love making people think they are fulfilling that need by cooking for them, providing material things, or entertaining them in some way. But in-between those good parts of them—and believe me, the conundrum is that the good parts are often just as intense as the bad parts because narcissists are almost ALWAYS very skilled and talented due to their intense drive for notoriety—in between the goodies is always the inevitable abuse. This is what allows for the proliferation of the narcissism virus.

The main ingredient is the hopelessness and stress felt by those who are dependent upon a narcissist with regard to getting their needs met. There is a point where you are absolutely worn out by catering to their needs, you realize you have completely abandoned your own needs, and coupled with the subconscious attraction we have to those who resemble the narcissist who has been abusing us and what those people are also doing to us, we lose all trust in the concept that anyone will ever care about our needs. Narcissists' demands REQUIRE that you abandon your own needs. We then DECIDE, that the only way we can get our needs met is to become completely self-centered and focus solely on our own needs. Fuck it. I'ma do ME.

The cycle then begins for the proliferation of our own narcissism. We decide that it is wise to begin to stop caring about other people so much. We decide that most people are assholes because we don't understand yet that we have been unconsciously conditioned to be extremely attracted to other narcissists. We are exhausted from constantly making sacrifices that go completely unappreciated. We feel totally alone, unappreciated, and under-valued. We have been conditioned by years of love and abuse, love and abuse, love and abuse. We have been so caught up in their patterns, their energy, their drama, and the constant chaos that thrives in their environment that we have forgotten who we are.

For the 'flight' types (like myself), we run far, far away, and engage in years of self-sabotaging behavior. But for the 'fight' types, the easiest way to survive is to become like them, because in that matrix, you can only meet violence with violence. It is stupid to bring a knife to a gun fight. Only guns work with guns. So you become argumentative, volatile, petty, defensive, harsh, callous, and self-centered—just like them.

What breaks my heart about this choice, is that the 'fight' types don't realize that this is exactly what the narcissist wants, because they live for the battle. This is why they are often such successful lawyers and CEO's; they are always ready for war! It is the only thing that makes them feel alive because they have lost the ability to experience joy. This also validates them. They love when their loved ones become like them, because it makes them right.

When others begin to function the same way the narcissists functions, it justifies their choices—the whole 'misery loves company' thing. You must become manipulative, dishonest, self-centered, and at least a tad opportunistic to get any of your needs met with a narcissist. This is the movie that is in their mind anyway, so you are just participating in it and this is great fun for them (you probably also get rewards for it, which is, as we said, a type of conditioning—an absolutely scientifically proved method of enforcing behavior).

This is a well-known outcome in any kind of abuse; the abused become the abuser. Men who tend to be physically abusive of women almost always come from a family where their mother was abused. This is why so many of those who are victims of narcissists will often become narcissists themselves, and it is a numbers game. It is a numbers game based on who will see the truth of who this person is and decide to make different choices, who will get away, who will tell others who this person really is, and who will either proliferate or end the cycle.

I was one of the 'internalizers,' so I suffered tremendously most of my life from illness and depression. I allowed feelings of extreme low self-worth to almost destroy me in my attempts to be a different person than my mother. Now let me say, I REALLY get why so many people make the opposite choice, play the game to preserve the status quo, and become like the narcissist. It has been an incredibly difficult life. It has been very lonely, very isolated, very painful, and I totally get why most would not want to feel the way I have felt and choose to avoid the inevitable fall-out of leaving the narcissists' side. Leaving always comes with a very heavy price, like losing loved ones (often an entire family). Everyone just isn't built to stand the pain of being without a tribe, so they will support the narcissist. Most of us will just keep quiet and do what we have to do to keep the security we have accumulated. Because narcissists are often such high-functioning people, there is a lot to lose. They generally acquire oodles of status and wealth, and it is difficult if you have lived under the comfort of their legacy to let go of that security.

I cannot count the number of nights I have cried myself to sleep. Shit, wailed actually. I have soaked through many pillows. I have tried to figure out how to live and be in excruciating pain. I have fallen on my knees in the dark begging to any God that could hear to take away my suffering. I have been racked with pain from head to toe from the sadness I have felt every year of my life for so many reasons that seemed to just keep repeating and repeating. I could not figure out what was wrong with me. I could not figure out why I couldn't find happiness.

After 45 years I started praying to be shown how to just make it to the end of my life so that I wouldn't hurt my daughter with my suicide. It's no joke to be raised by a narcissist. It will eventually destroy your life if you don't know what has happened to you and then seek some kind of healing. It is one of the most destructive viruses humankind has ever been plagued by, and the worst part about the sickness it creates, is that we don't even know that we have it. Most of us do not recognize the symptoms. Those who have decided to default to the 'you get yours and I'll get mine' mind-set are convinced it is the right way to be because in truth, that is what saved their life. Thus, many people are walking around with a virus that they have no idea they have.

Easy to control children

It's also very easy to pass this virus on to children. Their psychological immune systems haven't strengthened. They are very pliable and do not have a completely formed identity. Maybe we can call it low immunity to crazy! They have a great deal of neural plasticity, meaning their brains can easily be affected and influenced by external and internal stimuli. They almost automatically adjust to all circumstances.

Now, if and when the child of a narcissist tries to reject their own 'adjustment behavior' where they have figured out how to endure pain, and they begin to actually react to the pain being inflicted by the narcissist by standing up for themselves, like arguing and essentially fighting back, this is usually when the narcissist begins to really pile on the abuse, and you begin to fall out of favor with them. This is why things can be okay with a narcissist for a good amount of time when you are a child and have no choice but to do what you are told to survive. Children are easily pleased, and not sophisticated enough to challenge an adult's demands.

Once you become more self-sufficient however, and your personal needs turn out to be different than what works for the narcissist like, "I don't want to (eat/do/listen to/read/act like) this, life changes *forever*. It is very difficult for most of us to believe that the person who initially loved us so much and ensured our survival, will never do right by us again. The key to understanding this is that the reason they became a narcissist in the first place, is because THEY adjusted to someone not doing right by them. Thus, they have never done right by themselves. They don't even know what that looks like. How then could they possibly do right by you? It will only happen when you demand it, and because it is such a scary feeling to the narcissist to adjust to others, and thus very uncomfortable, they will just transfer all that horrible behavior to the next person willing to take it. After all, the one thing all of us want is comfort.

Whatever is comfortable for you, is what you will always pursue. Unfortunately, narcissists are most comfortable with stress. This is because when you have nothing else to think about, plan, work towards, do, or achieve, you are then forced to actually deal with your trauma. This is very uncomfortable to say the least, so it is preferable for many people to stay distracted with busy-ness and stress.

When you make the choice to stay in a relationship with a narcissist, whether parent/child, spouse, friend, or some other family member, it will deeply affect you, and maybe even change you drastically. You almost HAVE to become at least a little mean to communicate with them. This is because narcissists and those with narcissistic traits don't know how to interact with people without causing them pain, because they are in pain. They are addicted to wounding themselves and others, like an animal caught in a trap. It is a knee-jerk reaction to feeling pain, and they are always in pain. Upset. Mad. Pissed-off about something or feeling completely abandoned and misunderstood by everyone. They generally hide this in their public interactions, but it is quite clear in their private interactions.

When you are in relationship with a narcissist, you are always defending yourself or fighting back. In order to endure their constant slings and arrows, you must develop a level of emotional detachment and callousness, and this callousness will seep into your other relationships. This way of being can slowly mold you into a different person over time. And know this: it is a guarantee that if you are truly intimately involved with a narcissist or someone with narcissistic traits, you will lose a lot over time like money, relationships, your good health, and the ability to look at the world through positive and hopeful eyes. I have found most people to be very resistant to separating themselves from these relationships, usually because so much of your life is intertwined with them in material and emotional ways. But unfortunately, by the time people realize they must get away, they have usually suffered quite a bit, and lost quite a lot. Just take a look at almost ALL the people around Donald Trump … everyone is going down one by one.

Religion

Having already mentioned King James, Hitler, and Jim Jones, the discussion on narcissism would not be complete without an analysis of religion and its influence on the possibility of a narcissism epidemic. We've looked over micro-cosmic forces like relationship abuse and health, and we've looked at macro-cosmic forces like slavery and colonization, but what is a more powerful force in the lives of humans than the reason we are even here? Belief is probably the most powerful force that exists in the human makeup, and history has shown this time and again. Belief can lead to miracles or mayhem, and having control over the beliefs that populations and even small groups share has shown to bestow great power upon those who are able to manage those beliefs, as with the Pope or Jim Jones. This ability would certainly be attractive to anyone with NPD or who has narcissistic character traits.

Having the position of mediator between God and humans bestowed upon you could create a personality that assumes great personal importance. Without an abundance of maturity of character, this could, and often has, led to significant abuse of power. This has included violence (like with the Christian Holy Wars, the concept of Jihad associated with Islam, or the mass-suicides of cults), sexual abuse (like with the Catholic Church, Jesuit Priests in Africa, and Missionary's in the America's), and financial corruption (like with church's headed by greedy Evangelical Preachers in the U.S.). Religious Institutions like the Vatican and large church's in the U.S. and around the globe have great economic power and influence.

Religion is something that deeply affects the lives of millions of people. It seems to fulfill a human need, akin to the need for food and water. We have a need to acknowledge something outside of our material reality. The varied ways that we have come up with to "organize the universe" so to speak, to have some understanding of life and its overwhelming experiences, seems to be something that every group of people on this planet needs and continues to need. Providing this to people is an almost guaranteed position of importance. Anything that provides great personal importance is truly attractive to those with NPD or some of its characteristics. I mean, what's higher than worship?

To say that religious institutions are rife with narcissists is putting it mildly. The number of pedophiles in the Catholic Church alone is preposterous. Jim Jones is an extreme example of how far the violence can go. And by the way, I did research for an article I wrote on the Jonestown massacre and it was NOT a mass suicide, it was mass murder. It was captured on tape and attested to by 100's of witnesses that he forced those people at gun-point to drink that cyanide-laced Kool-Aid; they did not do it voluntarily[1]. In fact, one of the most devout members, Sharon Amos, killed her two children by stabbing them to death at Jones' command; this is how afraid of being exposed as a fraud this narcissist was. He preferred dying and killing everyone around him so there was no one to tell the truth, to it being exposed that his commune was a disaster and that the people were living in terrible conditions[2], all in the name of God. When you have identified so completely with your public persona that you cannot bear to let it go and will sacrifice human lives to do that, you have become a monster. A monster lurking inside a human being.

There are many, many historical accounts from indigenous people around the world of the sexual, physical, mental, and emotional abuse from Christian Missionaries. Malidoma Patrice Some talks about it in his book *Of Water and the Spirit* (1994). There is a heart-wrenching documentary called *We Were Children* (2012) about the sexual, physical, and emotional abuse of Indigenous children kidnapped from their tribes at the behest of priests starting in the late 1800's; they were forced to attend 'Indian Boarding Schools' here in the U.S. The last schools closed in the 1990's and this occurred for 125 years with an estimated 180,000 Indigenous children having been abducted[3].

One of the most damning portraits that I have seen is from the HBO documentary *Mea Maxima Culpa: Silence in the House of God* (2012). It relates the story of four deaf men who were victims of sexual abuse at the hands of Father Lawrence Murphy, director of the St. Johns School for the Deaf in Milwaukee, Wisconsin. They were all raped when they were boys, and the facts in the following 2 paragraphs are taken from this documentary:

This is apparently the first known case of sexual abuse charges against the Catholic Church in the U.S. to be tried in court, and it eventually reached across continents, even sparking victims in Ireland to add their complaints. It went all the way to the top of the Vatican. Pope John Paul II and the following Pope Benedict XVI were in office at the time. It is at least known that Murphy, who was an active clergy member from 1950 to 1975, abused numerous deaf boys, always choosing those who could not sign yet so that they were unable to tell anyone, from his appointment as director in 1963. The details of how he was able to get away with it include a combination of two characteristics of this narcissistic epidemic: 1) sophisticated methods of manipulation, and 2) systemic support. When at his yearly retreat to his summer cabin with a group of boys from St. Johns, he would make the older boys who had already been abused choose which younger boy would sleep with him on a given night. This made them complicit, and thus much less likely to confide in someone. He told one of the boys not to bother telling his mother because his mother didn't love him, only loved his elder brother who had died. This particular man shared in the documentary that he had also personally been reluctant to tell his mother because not only had his brother died from electrocution, his father had committed suicide and he did not want to add to his mother's pain. This is an example of how predators work, choosing the most vulnerable prey. Another man admitted that he even felt special that he was being 'chosen' by someone who was so important. Clearly, the nuns looked the other way, and upon reflection as adults, when sharing their stories with each other, the men realized there was no way the nuns did not know. Out of desperation, one of the boys had actually told a visiting priest what was happening in confession and later witnessed a verbal altercation between that priest and Father Murphy. That priest never came back. When these four boys became adults and discovered after sharing their stories that Murphy was still molesting, they posted fliers with a picture of his face around Milwaukee revealing his pedophile practices and warning parents to protect their children. It reached the archdiocese, Murphy actually confessed, and he was sent away to a 'retreat' for a few weeks, after which he returned and apparently continued to abuse boys. The four men also went to the police, who did nothing. The accusations made it all the way to the D.A.'s office—again, nothing was done. By 1974, the evidence against Murphy was over-whelming and he left St. Johns for 'health reasons', was given a tearful send-off hailing him as a hero in the community in a lavish ceremony thanking him and celebrating him with applause, tears, and hugs. He was then re-assigned to a local church named St. Anne's whose members knew nothing of his charges, where he continued to molest. All of this documented abuse had been consistently delivered to the Vatican Ambassador in D.C. so that by 1974, they had known about it for over 20 years.

The practice of merely sending priests who had sexually abused away on a retreat for 'spiritual treatment' goes back to 1947 with the Order of the Paraclete in Jemez Springs, New Mexico. It was opened by Father Gerald Fitzgerald who ironically, believed these priests should be removed from service. He constantly wrote to Bishops and the Pope telling them that the Catholic Church was 'infested' with pedophilia. He spent $80 million treating more than 2000 sexual predator priests in centers in Italy, France, Great Britain, Africa, South America, and the Philippines. The centers provided absolutely no psychological counseling or medical help; the priests were simply forced to pray on their knees for hours at a time, pleading for mercy. A former Benedictine Monk, Patrick J. Wall from St. Johns Abbey in Collegeville, Minnesota, who was given the assignment to travel the country removing molesters and relocating them, reported that there were 55 molesters in one monastery, more than 70 in the archdiocese, and was given authorization to settle for up to $250,000 if he could get a confidentiality order from the parents of abused children. In 1995, he had a budget of $7 million. Once he realized there were no efforts at reformation, only removal and relocation, he left the priesthood. Ultimately, Father Murphy never paid for his crimes, and was buried with all priestly honors in the Church Cemetery. By the time Attn. Jeff Anderson filed over 1500 lawsuits against the Vatican by 2010, the case had gotten the attention of journalists, other ethical priests, and the community of accusers in Ireland who had complained about pedophilia in the Catholic Church for decades. One of the worst cases was on Priest Tony Walsh from Lady of the Assumption Church in Dublin, who was a notorious pedophile having committed by his own admission, over 200 acts of abuse. Again, parents had continually notified the Police and the Vatican for over 20 years—nothing was done. He was also sent to the Paraclete for a short time, relocated to another Church, and continued to abuse children. The Vatican unceasingly ordered the vow of omertà, the famous Mafia code of silence, to anyone in the church who attempted to intercede on behalf of these abused children, with the threat of excommunication if they disobeyed. Meanwhile in Milwaukee, a priest charged with handling the public accusations of sexual abuse moved $55 million in Church assets to a cemetery trust, and the archdiocese declared bankruptcy so that no victims could be paid any damages. Boston lost more than 50% of its parishes, and cases have been brought against the Catholic Church now in Latin America, the Philippines, Africa, and India. The cherry on top of the whole scandal was the revelation that the largest fundraiser for the Vatican and the Catholic Church around the globe, Martial Maciel Degollado, who founded the Legion of Christ in 1941, opened seminaries and universities around the world, controlled an annual operating budget of $650 million, and is associated with people like Carlos Slim (the richest man in the world), Jeb Bush, former chairman of Citigroup Bank Sandy Weill, and former CIA Director William Casey, *was a brutal sex criminal*. This man, who was dearly loved by Pope John Paul II, was a morphine addict, abused dozens of boys in his organization by insisting on being masturbated by a boy or anally raping them anytime he visited, had mistresses and multiple children whom he also molested. When these stories surfaced, they were ignored, he was never arrested, and he remained close to the Vatican until two years before his death. The details in this documentary were among many other stories that support my assertion of the extreme level of narcissism in the Catholic

Church. Journalist Robert Mickens from The Tablet-Catholic Weekly said, "I still hear some of the old monsignor in the Vatican saying 'Well, you know, boys have always done this in all-male environments. It's normal. This wasn't abuse … these kids, they were interested and it's rites of passage." —in 2011! Another Bishop is quoted as saying "Little boys heal; they will get over it." He was referring to a priest who had molested numerous boys between the ages of 10 and 13 by anally raping them. A therapist who examined Father Murphy determined that he was untreatable because he felt he was 'fixing' the boys:

> *"There was rampant homosexuality among the older boys. I fixed the problem. I thought if I'd play around with a kid once per week, they would have their needs met. I thought I was taking their sins on myself. It was sex education for them. They were confused about sex. If their penis was erect, I would masturbate them, afterward I prayed and went to confession."*

One of the most poignant moments in the documentary is when it is pointed out that the radio signals from the Vatican are so strong, you can hear Sunday morning mass through your doorbell, yet the church has been completely silent about all the accusations of sexual abuse. In the end, 50,000 pages of documents were found in the Vatican from as early as 1700 showing sex abuse with children. As said in the documentary, "Belief in God inspires loyalty to sociopaths."

Being in position as a connection to God seems to require a combination of required sacrifices, along with great power and access to resources. This combination produces a duality inside of a human being that is another form of the experience of abuse and privilege.

Clearly many human beings are not able to completely give up sex. So, you cannot openly enjoy a healthy sex life, but you are in circumstances where you can get it privately and force secrecy so that you are able to hold on to your powerful position and source of security. This powerful position results in other forms of abuse as well, such as pressuring people to remain in abusive marriages, not use birth control, or be subservient in some way to other human beings. There are also the social abuses that result from church's having far-reaching influence over governments and financial institutions to spend money on and cater to a certain sector of the population—again, in the name of God. A good example of this is the plot for *The Godfather Part 3* (1990).

Perhaps it's the inclusion/ostracization factor inherent in belief that separates us from one-another due to clashing values, which creates an inherent atmosphere of conflict that religion seems to have been embroiled in for thousands of years …

At any rate, it takes individual people to stand in these powerful roles, and those that would want to live this kind of life, in service to God, would understandably have a very unique character. Having that much influence over other human beings is a great responsibility and would be equally motivated by either altruistic or purely egotistical motives. It can also be a healthy combination of both, producing a flawed but well-intentioned character, and this is what most people expect and tend to see because, well, this is what we are taught to see. We have not always inherently been taught to be on alert for the pathologies in people, especially people with status. Low expectations for abuses of power is something that is ideologically conditioned in us regarding religious people, and this nurtures an environment that makes it very easy for them to get away with exactly that.

There are certainly many healthy aspects of religion such as inner peace, social inclusion, support, belonging, and connections that provide comfort and deep meaning to life, all of which nurtures positive well-being. Unfortunately, how important these things are to human beings makes providing them attractive to narcissists. At this point we must evolve our thinking. We must acknowledge that it is important to remain objective about who people in positions of power really are, and be open to our own capacity for over-looking things in our zeal to hold on to our comfortable expectations. Or our money.

Who pt. 2

"You're a monster!" Dracula: "And you're a lawyer, nobody's perfect." - Dracula (Netflix/2020)

From priests to politicians, it is crucial that we learn to identify who the narcissists are, and who is the most vulnerable to them. Narcissists would not be able to behave in the way they do if we were not putting up with them. The person who is taking or being subjected to their abuse is necessary for the abuser to function, and those of us who are 'taking it' so to speak, are a special category of people who also have certain characteristics. These are the co-dependent, enabler types and I am intimately acquainted with that concept having been one of them, as have so many of you, and I can look back now and say yep! that's me.

But first, let's start with who the narcissists are. Since narcissism is required for psychopathy, looking at trends with psychopaths is relevant to NPD. Here is a list of the top 10 job titles that research has shown to have the highest numbers of anti-social personalities (specifically psychopaths):

1.   CEO
2.   Lawyer
3.   Media person in TV or radio
4.   Salesperson
5.   Surgeon
6.   Journalist
7.   Police Officer
8.   Clergy Person
9.   Chef
10. Civil Servant

I find it quite interesting that all of these jobs are positions of service to others. I know a large percentage of jobs are about service to others, but these days many of them are not. Many job positions are just about being in service to a company, like accounting, recruiting, maintenance, or marketing. Many positions now do not require much interaction with the public, but every single career in the above list does indeed require significant interaction with the public, and in very crucial ways that determine a persons' health, freedom, livelihood and even their life. The key word is 'important' when it comes to what narcissists want to be. I also believe that it is much easier for anti-social personalities to hide in certain positions because no one will suspect them.

We are not as informed as a society quite yet on the true nature of mental illness like say, the way we have increased our understanding of physics. Here in the Western world, we understand many more scientific principles about the universe now than we did 400 years ago, and while our understanding and treatment of what we call mentally ill has progressed, we still think of someone who is mentally ill as very obviously dysfunctional and incapable of normalcy. You know, crazy. *This is seriously un-true.*

There are many, many high-functioning and seemingly normal mentally ill people like Ted Bundy or John Wayne Gacy. The mind is apparently just as complex as the universe, and I have always felt that basic principles of psychology should be taught in high school, considering the large number of serial killers we have seen in the last 100 years or so of our history. I counted 111 just in the 1970's on Wikipedia! This is even more poignant considering how many mentally ill people become parents. I don't think there is any more important position in a person's life than parent. Parents are the shapers of society since they are shaping the minds of the people who make up our society. Parent is not on the sociopath job list because it is not considered a career, but I suggest it is even more important than a career.

The main person left off of that list is of course criminal, but any one of those positions can also be criminals, and unfortunately for us many of them are. Ted Bundy was studying to be a lawyer, Rodney Alcala got on TV when he did a dating show, and we probably don't need to go into the Police category any further as I am sure we are all aware at this point (thanks to movies and cell-phone footage) just how criminal police officers can be. The latest serial killer, Joseph J. DeAngelo (The Golden State Killer), was in fact a police officer. At this point there are so many famous people that I now identify with NPD like the boxing promoter Don King, Richard Nixon and the Kardashians, but I have also unfortunately personally known a lot of people that I am pretty convinced have NPD such as social workers, cops, teachers, bosses, and folk in the entertainment business. Sadly, I have had the most contact with narcissists in interacting with my own family …

Ok. Now to those most vulnerable. If those are the top positions for anti-social personalities (such as psychopaths and narcissists), then I suppose the most vulnerable to them would be the people they serve and are in charge of. That would thus include consumers, job seekers, accused and convicted criminals, those with illnesses or in need of healthcare, anyone that is a part of news-worthy attention, churchgoers, restaurant workers, and those in need of social services like soldiers with PTSD, the homeless, the handicapped, the elderly, or foster kids. In the case of the history of our country, I would add women, anyone with a sexual orientation that is condemned, people of color (especially descendants of slaves and indigenous peoples), animals, and the earth itself. This list basically encompasses anyone in need, and anything at the mercy of human behavior.

Needs are what narcissists feed off of, as well as many of our desires, which are deeply affected by our needs! You don't need coffee, but you do need energy. You don't need a cigarette, but you do need to stay calm. Oh—and the cigarette industry is such a perfect example of the outcome of narcissism—they have just freely been selling death to people for decades now. People like the lobbyist character who was the star of *Thank You For Smoking* (2005) played by Aaron Eckhart—classic narcissist!

Now to really bring it on home, those who are the most vulnerable in our society, are also the most vulnerable to anti-social personalities. Animal predators carefully choose prey based on who is in a position of weakness such as being separated from their mother or the pack, being small, or in some way without protection, and it is those of us that need the most help who are often the victims of anti-social personalities, which are human predators. They are often in charge because they are extremely ambitious and motivated to achieve.

A key component in my assertion of a narcissism epidemic is that there are a lot of narcissists making very important decisions including who gets hired, who gets fired, what kind of medicine you get and how much you pay for it (creepy-ass Martin Shkreli), and whether or not you can get fair and humane treatment in our so-called advanced, modern, civil society. I suggest that as long as we have anti-social personality types in charge of our world, we have not yet reached the status of being able to call ourselves a 'civil' society. We are working on it though! And I believe we will improve with greater understanding.

The Impact

"All there is, is bullshit. Layers of it. One layer on top of another … You pick the layer of bullshit you prefer, and that's your bullshit." - Bernie LaPlante (Dustin Hoffman), Hero (1992)

From Khalil Gibran's *The Prophet* (1923), to Charles Dickens' novels, to Hollywood blockbusters like *Little Big Man* (1970) and *One Flew Over the Cuckoo's Nest* (1975), to the TV series *Roots* (1977), to the documentary craze on today's digital networks like Netflix and Prime, art and literature have been trying to address many societal problems that we have been plagued with for quite a while now. Bob Marley wrote in his song *War* (1976) "until the philosophy which hold's one race superior, and another inferior, is finally and permanently discredited and abandoned, everywhere is war." Mother Theresa, Princess Di, M.L.K., Ghandi, Krishnamurti, Ella Baker, Fred Hampton, and Malcolm X are among the many concerned souls that have addressed the issues of poverty, hunger, racism, and societal corruption that have been a scourge on humankind for some time now. It is no exaggeration to state that the world has been moving rapidly towards a serious state of physical and biological imbalance for a few centuries. To say that our planet is not in the greatest condition is an under-statement. Industrialization, pollution, corporate monopolies, and worsening health care and living circumstances for millions of people around our globe is proof of this narcissism epidemic I am claiming. There simply aren't enough caring, honest, compassionate, emotionally healthy people IN CHARGE. Why?

Because us caring types aren't willing to use violence to maintain power. I honestly believe it is that simple.

It has always amazed me how the level of violence used on the slaves and Indigenous people in the U.S. and in all colonized countries is never a significant topic in the conversation when discussing the state of those oppressed people and the conditions they are in. Torture is something that will utterly destroy a human being's capacity for healthy functioning. The methods and degrees of violence used on all these colonized people has been extreme (check out *Exterminate All the Brutes* (2020) on HBO), and this affects multiple generations of the descendants of those subjected to it, as well as the descendants of those who were doing the subjecting. I mean, I totally get that we don't want to traumatize children while educating them, but very few of us are ever taught about some of the details of slavery and colonization like the consistent rape, psychological torture, violent abuse, and systematic oppression that on a daily basis occurred year after year for centuries. The Indigenous inhabitants of these colonized countries would have had to almost transform into psychopaths overnight to defend themselves.

Let's take a minute to really address this phenomenon holistically. There is ample attention paid to the victim status of those who are on the receiving end of abuse, but few of us consider the vulnerability of those who are witness to the abuse, and/or who are encouraged or conditioned to behave in those awful ways. If a child is raised to believe that torture is acceptable, or at least a normal part of existence, and they are encouraged to be violent and abusive themselves, they are being set up for a life that will most likely not progress or end well. **That 'end well' part is really hidden from us!**

We are all witness to the advantages that those in power have and the ways this seems to make their lives much easier and quite privileged. We see the limos, the mansions, the diamonds, and all the excess lifestyle, but you really have to dig deep or pay close attention to the stories that reveal how devastating the personal lives are of those who have amassed great fortune, which is often from something that has caused massive suffering.

I spoke earlier on Leo Baekland, the inventor of plastics, a material that is causing great destruction to our planet because it is not bio-degradable, and how Baekeland's grandson murdered his own mother and eventually killed himself. His mother had sex with him in an attempt to turn him from gay to straight, and he later stabbed her to death. He was put in a mental institution, released to his Grandmother who he also stabbed but didn't kill, and he eventually committed suicide by (poetically) putting a plastic bag over his head and smothering himself. I have also mentioned all the

Shakespearean stories of the horrific things that go on inside the castle walls of Kings and Queens, as well as the history of real live Kings and Queens who benefitted from slavery and war, and their eventual descent into madness and agonizing death. Other notable examples are Dick Cheney and his 7 open-heart surgeries, the real estate heir and murderer Robert Durst witnessing his mother's suicide when he was a child, the suicides of German billionaires Adolf Merckle and Otto Beisheim, and the kidnapping and torture of J. Paul Getty's grandson which led to his heroin addiction and eventual death after decades of confinement in a wheelchair[5]. Other heroin tragedies include the deaths from over-dose of oil billionaire T. Boone Pickens' grandson, the daughter of millionaire David Siegel, and the daughter-in-law of Swedish millionaire Hans Rausing[6].

The U.S. has many tragic examples of the suffering of very wealthy people in the stories of Johnson & Johnson heiress Casey Johnson, Southern Pacific Railroad heiress Edie Sedgwick, Gloria Vanderbilt's son Carter, Aristotle Onassis's daughter Christina, tobacco heiress Doris Duke, and hotel heiress Francesca Hilton—most of whom died quite young, but all very tragically[7].

These are just a few examples, but if you really pay attention to bio- and autobiographical film and literature, you will see that there are a great number of tragic stories associated with the very wealthy. There may be a connection between this and the fact that unfortunately, as I have been suggesting, most great wealth has been procured through the suffering of human beings.

By the way, did you notice how the majority of the tragedy impacts the children, descendants, and spouses of those descendants of the person who made the fortune, rather than the actual person who made the fortune? The sins of the fathers …. the sinking ship … Karma … what goes around comes around … all of this is the science of behavior.

In terms of what these wealthy men have done that would justify my pointing out the significance of wealth and suffering, the businesses that these people ran to acquire their great wealth included drilling into the earth for toxic oil, selling people cigarettes and pharmaceuticals (opiates) and the now ocean-infesting plastic, and businesses that have made their fortune from under-paying and over-working it's employees like the railroads and coal mines. *There Will Be Blood* (2007) starring Daniel Day-Lewis is a great narrative for this concept. The amount of stress, illness, and tragedy that these businesses have caused to masses of people who worked in them over time is unfathomable. I would imagine this is especially true for the business of someone like Dick Cheney who funds wars (Halliburton), and I find it quite interesting how much the families of these entrepreneurs seem to have suffered, particularly from addiction and mental health issues.

The main point I am making here, is not so much that things are worse for the rich, but that they are not necessarily better. Thanks to reality TV, it is clear that all of these things happen in all families whether poor, middle class, or rich, and the bottom line is that ultimately, wealth does not protect you from mental illness. And to be clear, I am suggesting that all of these people who made their fortune off of and caused so much of other people's suffering and pain, were probably narcissistic to some degree considering their comfort with causing other people's suffering.

As I will continue to point out, physical and mental health are significantly impacted by stress, and this shows in for example, the high rates of cancer, diabetes and addiction in the African American community. It does appear though, that in order to win, be victorious, get the prize, or be successful, you have to be willing to inflict a considerable amount of pain and misery. And the outcome of all this misery? A LOT of miserable people, mass self-hatred, trauma, addiction, and poor health; high numbers of people who, as Alfred said in *Batman: The Dark Knight* (2008), "just want to watch the world burn" are now living amongst us. The list of serial killers, psychopaths and sociopaths, and those with mental illness is extensive to say the least. What this produces in a general sense, is a society full of people who are unable to experience joy.

I really believe this is the true bugger: The inability to experience joy. Narcissists only find joy in conflict, and specifically in being victorious in conflict. I did have moments of joy in my childhood, but many of the moments that are traditionally associated with fun and good times unfortunately were not joyful for me. For instance, my mother seemed to love to pick dinnertime to vent her narcissistic rage. The feeling of crying, how poofy and sore your eyes and your face feel, how tight your gut feels, the snot coming out of your nose, the process of trying to chew and swallow food with a dry mouth and how it loses its taste and feels like hot liquid rubber going down your throat is such a familiar feeling to me. I could never get through a meal, would wind up leaving the table before cleaning my plate, and so was often hungry at night. I had to learn to fall asleep with a growling belly, so being in a state of hunger was something I became numb to after a while. Thus, my own discomfort in general is something I was conditioned to become numb to after a while. I would rather leave the dinner table as a child than risk getting popped in the middle of the forehead, screamed at, or having some fun thing taken away like going outside to play. Not eating became an escape. Of course it makes sense that I have been fighting an eating disorder my entire life. At 49 years old I weighed about 112 pounds. The worst of this disorder was when I was in my early 20's, and my weight plummeted to 80 pounds after I remembered everything that had happened to me and proceeded to descend into a terrible state of illness which lasted for over 20 years.

This was the turning point in my life. I had gone home to what was about the 10th or 11th house that we lived in during a break from college, which at that time was in Virginia. I was home alone, looking through a photo album, and I found a polaroid in the very back, turned over, of my mom in lingerie. It was very sexual, and when I turned the photo over, there was writing on the back that I recognized as my sisters' handwriting. It was quite evident to me that my sister had taken the picture (and she confirmed this later), and this was so disturbing to me that I suddenly began to have a flashback of my mother forcing me to watch her give herself a vaginal exam. I started kind of hyper-ventilating, remembering how awful it was for me to have to observe her poking around her private parts, and realizing that she had exposed me and my little sister to very inappropriate sexual situations. I remembered walking in on my mom having sex several times with different men, and how my stepfather would walk around naked, and how he would force me to strip naked to give me beatings, which my mother was aware of. I began stumbling around the house, touching paintings on the wall and just remembering, remembering, remembering. Remembering all the beatings, the punishments, the verbal berating. It was overwhelming and I collapsed in a heap.

I eventually called my Grandmother sobbing, and she said, "Oh thank God." She had been patiently waiting over the years for me to remember the things that had happened to me, many of which she did not even know about, but she knew my mother was a narcissist, and she knew that I had probably suffered tremendously.

There was also the more covert neglect like never taking me to the doctor, which has left me with certain conditions to this day that cause me discomfort. My mother generally ignored my pain, so I had to ignore my pain. She ignored my hunger, so I ignored my hunger. But I tell you, she didn't ignore when I messed up—now THAT got attention. If I missed a spot on the counter while cleaning the kitchen, or ate candy, or didn't do well on a test, or didn't clean up after myself, or came home late from playing outside, or just had a need that she didn't want to deal with in the moment, there was all kinds of attention given in those moments to my 'self-centeredness.' No matter how hard I tried to be absolutely perfect, there was ALWAYS something wrong; some reason for her to be angry.

When I finally did escape to college, she would send me 10-page tirade letters (front and back) about how selfish I was and all the responsibilities she had and all the things she had to do in response to when I would ask her to pay my tuition so that I could register for classes. Just to put it into perspective, I had a scholarship, only had about $1000 left over to pay, and she was a fully employed professor at the time.

There was simply very little joy in my household as a child. There was laughter because my mother was hilarious; she was very smart and very witty. There were very few actual joyful times though, where there was a feeling of connectedness and love. After she and my sister's father separated, there was a parade of men that came through my life as my mother's love and sex addiction just got completely out of hand. All of these relationships were racked with conflict, stress, and turmoil. It's so embarrassing to constantly run into one of your mother's lovers ...

Once I was able to get away from home as a young adult, I immediately discovered that the way I lived my own life, without my mother's influence, was much more peaceful and drama-free, but I did not ever really feel good inside. I was always suffering immensely within my close relationships, and feelings of abandonment, rejection, and low self-esteem have plagued me my entire life.

As I get older, I have begun to be more aware of certain thoughts and responses I have within the context of my relationships that are just. so. CRAZY. There is always an underlying sense of extreme fear, danger, or disappointment. As soon as I would begin to really care about someone, I began to have terrifying thoughts of abandonment and rejection. I start imagining all the horrible things they might do that would devastate me, remembering times from my youth when that happened. It has always been a painful experience being in a relationship because I would become quickly attached to someone, but know deep down inside that the relationship would eventually come to an end. I realize now with more wisdom, that the reason for that tendency to developing a quick attachment, is that when you have experienced so much pain and trauma in relationships with those you love, it is over-whelming to feel the pleasure of someone being kind to you, and you do not want it to end. It becomes like a fix for pain and can have the same addictive outcomes as substance dependency.

I feel so much more laid back and free now, but it has been a really torturous state to be in; it is very stressful and exhausting. I am fairly positive at this point in my development that the high levels of cortisol my body has produced over the years from fear, stress, and loss has put a toll on certain organs in my body, especially my bladder and intestines. I have had numerous digestive issues, bladder and kidney infections, and mysterious pains. I have had consistent sleeping disorders including nightmares, sleepwalking, and insomnia. I have suffered from severe depression, an eating disorder, anxiety, and had panic attacks. I have endured decades of nerve and muscle pain from untreated injuries and structural pathologies with my spine. It has been so very hard to just feel good. Joy has been an elusive friend, and this seems to be the case for so many of us hampered by a dysfunctional upbringing and the ensuing long-term effects. The impact on people in a society built and powered on narcissism is massive self-hatred, wide-spread abuse, and the inability for people to experience and feel real joy, which stimulates cycles and epidemics of addiction, mental illness, high rates of morbidity, and suicidal behavior.

Chapter 5

THE RESPONSE

"Momma you can choose the rain, but I choose the Sun. That's all I need to free myself." -Nikka Costa, So Have I For You (2001)

Introduction

One of the most poignant responses to a narcissist I have ever seen are the final words from the Judge to Ted Bundy at the end of his trial which were "Take care of yourself son." These are the words of a man who is an authority figure in the highest sense of the word as he is charged with deciding people's fate and freedom, talking to a person who has brutally raped, murdered and maimed dozens of young women. His choice was to show Bundy some affection and care! It seems this was based on his opinion that Bundy was a "bright young man" and had wasted his talents.

That the Judge had any thoughts that his words would have any significant impact on this psychopathic serial killer is testament to all the information I have shared pointing to how much our cultural tendencies and the very foundation of our society have supported and often nurtured the proliferation of narcissism. Ted Bundy was studying to be that second item on the list of careers with the most psycho/sociopaths (lawyer), and even in the face of being accused of the most heinous crime's possible, was afforded respect as a result of his ambitions.

President Donald Trump stated clearly on video that you can quickly find on YouTube, that he could shoot someone on 5th Avenue and not lose any voters. This is a big part of the world we live in. The individualism has reached a level of absurdity to where it doesn't matter what you do, only how much notoriety you have achieved or how much money you have acquired. This level of privilege used to seem to be more outwardly reserved for those born into positions of power or those who were able to leverage their relationship with those in positions of power. It can now be afforded to the common person with access to any of the numerous platforms available to anyone with a cell phone or laptop.

I do want to address this issue of what 'used to be' briefly, because it has occurred to me that the phrase 'there is nothing new under the sun' also has a good bit of legitimacy. I do believe it is true that there is very little human behavior that is brand new. We have been here quite a long time now. Based on many of the preserved histories of different cultures, the legacy of literature from at least the last 1000 years, and the many films we have of the last 100 years or so depicting humankind's numerous atrocities, there have always been rapists, murderers, thieves and general madness and insanity. There has been a lot of war, a lot of violence, and therefore most likely a lot of narcissism. It may be that there is no more today than there ever was, and we are just more privy to the evidence of it because of technology, but I would argue that this may be the very reason for increasing cases of narcissism, because as previously mentioned, human beings do tend towards copy-catting.

Since the U.S. actually elected a President with a raging case of NPD (even though he did not get the most votes!), maybe we can at least agree that there is certainly an over-all growing, or at least continuing acceptance of and even high regard for narcissistic personalities. From Hitler to Harvey Weinstein, there certainly seems to be quite a few famous and successful narcissists. Since fame is now a much more available commodity, I suggest there are a lot more common folk with narcissistic tendencies as well.

We are literally having an explosion of fame, so it is becoming a new normal. This being the case, our general response to narcissists has been lack-luster. Those of us who just have your average cocktail of normal human weaknesses and faults, but who are generally trying our best and actually care about others, find it difficult and in my experience often impossible to really conceive of a human being who truly does not have the capability to authentically empathize with another human being. In fact, I have known many people who are utterly resistant to this concept. They literally will not consider that they cannot ever work out their problems with certain people and that there is no solution that will eventually help to create a healthy relationship. They believe to their imminent destruction that this person can and will eventually change, and that they should not give up on them. It is very difficult for us to accept that certain personality changes are permanent.

It is a mystery why one person who is abused grows up to be a champion for children's rights, and another person who is abused grows up to be an abuser themselves. There is some kind of cocktail of environment, experiences, and personal make-up that pushes each of us in a particular direction, but I have experienced repeatedly that those of us who lean towards the light have a difficult time accepting that this is not the case for others, and that it never will be.

I will continually point out that the medical consensus is that NPD does not have a cure. Psychiatrists will promote therapy, and they will say that it can help, but you will not find one saying they have cured NPD. The damage those with NPD cause is compounded by the high esteem with which our society regards certain types of people. Not only have we not recognized who they really are, we have worshipped narcissists. It is understandable, and as pontificated upon earlier, the cause for this goes way back into human history. But this lack-luster response has now become something integrated into our daily interactions, rather than only applying to someone who is larger than life like say, a King or an Emperor. The character traits possessed by people like Hitler, Mussolini, or the most prolific African Slave-Trader Tippu-Tip, such as a complete lack of consideration for humanity, is now very common-place. Certain types of people have become more and more common over time. The Bible certainly has numerous examples of sociopaths and narcissists, the Nazi's took it to a momentous level, and the last few decades have seen many insane cult leaders.

Now, NPD is everywhere. They are police, lawyers, and family members. The normalization of this personality type is also very evident when you see the social structures of certain groups of people like the Iroquois (composed of 6 nations) who had instead normalized compassion and care within the structure of their society[1]. The list of serial killers, psychopaths, and murderous dictators has grown quite long over the centuries, but I fear our ability to curb certain types of behavior is diminishing because increasingly larger numbers of the general population aspire to that type of greatness. So unfortunately, we admire people who are secretly ruthless.

They often have great power over others, especially financial power, because they are often the boss. They decide whether you get and keep the job. Since everyone needs the job to survive, allowing narcissists to behave in the maniacal ways that they do is pretty much a survival tactic. Very few people want to risk their livelihood or their life to expose a corrupt person, and let's be honest, there is a good reason for this fear. It does appear that people who stand up against oppression are often cut down, like Sandra Bland, Malcolm X, Spartacus, and Gary Webb (who apparently committed suicide by shooting himself in the head TWICE, yep, after exposing governmental corruption related to the crack epidemic in the U.S.). This fear has now translated into a type of social etiquette, so that people are easily conditioned into accepting unkind treatment at the least, and brutal treatment at the worst. The recent police killing of George Floyd and the dozens of other Black men and women murdered by police is an integral and consistent part of the legacy of the brutal murders of African Americans by White Americans in positions of authority in the U.S., and even though many of the murders are filmed from beginning to end, there is question of culpability. This is how confident that narcissistic cop was that he could probably get away with it. This is because cops have gotten away with it for over 400 years. African Americans have been enduring police brutality since being brought here in chains, and for the community of descendants of those enslaved, it is normal.

The sad truth is that many of us have known very little outside of unkind treatment since we were born, and we have all silently sanctioned it by justifying the behavior of brutal people and justifying our own tolerance of it. When something is normal to you, what more would you expect? How can you want something you don't even know about? It you have never had a banana, you will never have a craving for a banana. If you've never known kindness, your very survival depends on you finding a way to be ok with that. So, what most of us do in the face of being in a relationship with a narcissist, is find ways to manage it. Because in comparison to the way the rest of the world is behaving, they may not seem that bad. Just as groups of people like slaves and prisoners have adjusted to their oppression, many people spend their entire lives adjusting to and managing relationships with narcissists. This is mainly because for the most part, in terms of the most toxic aspects of their character, those with NPD do not change. They may alter their behavior, adjust to changing circumstances, and perfect their manipulation tactics, but due to the low level of treatment for NPD, they actually usually just get worse with time, just like with any other untreated illness.

Is there a cure?

So far, the scientific consensus is that there is no cure for NPD. This is according to several medical resources including WebMD, The Mayo Clinic, and quite a few published doctors like Dr. Ramani Durvasula, and Dr. Daniel Fox who will both tell you that there is definitely treatment available, but you will not hear them say there is a cure[2].

Most therapists do claim that talk-therapy can help and that change is possible, but this is very tricky territory considering that they also admit that most narcissists are not even capable of admitting they have a problem that could use treatment, thus they generally do not engage in any talk-therapy. I have yet to find a recorded example of a therapist claiming they have cured a narcissist. In fact, there is a school of thought that talk-therapy may even nurture NPD.

One of my favorite takes on this concept is from what is in my opinion the greatest show ever on narcissism, *The Sopranos* (1999), in Season 6, pt.2, Episode 8. The psychiatrist (Dr. Melfi) who has been treating the violent Mafia mob boss (Tony Soprano) for years for what started out as his panic attacks, but slowly morphed into her realization that he has NPD, is reading a book by a fellow psychiatrist on the efficacy of talk-therapy on narcissists. Earlier in the episode she was at a dinner with colleagues and the discussion turned to studies on criminals and how they are able to discuss lofty subjects, appear engaged and even caring, but make no change in their behavior. One of the dinner guests suggests that talk-therapy actually assists criminals in their criminal enterprises because it helps them perfect their manipulation techniques. The friends cite what I have found out are actual real books on anti-social personalities including *The Criminal Personality* (1976) by Stanton Samenow and Samuel Yochelson. Later that evening Dr. Melfi is in bed reading this book, and a paragraph from it has a profound impact on her: "The criminal's sentimentality reveals itself in compassion for babies and pets. The criminal uses insight to justify heinous acts. Therapy has potential for non-criminals; for criminals it becomes one more criminal operation[3]." Realizing that Soprano is doing this with her, she refers him to another doctor at their next session and ends her treatment of him.

She realized what is true about those with NPD, which is that even when it appears they are trying to change, they are not trying to change. They are just pretending in order to keep the food supply around. Like Vampires. This is what everyone around a narcissist is. Food supply.

Narcissistic Supply

There are supplies that we all need; toilet paper, cooking oil, water, and clothes are just a few. Narcissists' main supply need in addition to these things is OTHER PEOPLE'S ENERGY. The common clinical term for this is narcissistic supply. Those with NPD were depleted of their own personal life energy years ago as a result of abuse and/or neglect, and the main reason they engage in any kind of relationship is to siphon energy from another person. This is in line with what I feel is a great metaphorical equivalent to narcissists, vampires.

I have a theory that much of the mythology of many ancient cultures involving monsters or other destructive beings is really about the horrible things that human beings can become, and the vampire narrative is extremely parallel to that of narcissists. Think about it—they are always depicted as beautiful, sexy, enticing, powerful, and desirable. They have power over people just using their voice. They are alive, but dead, and need human blood to survive, so they are predators and really have no true regard for anyone.

Narcissists need human energy; this is part of the reason why they are so ambitious. They need the accolades and admiration of other people to feel any kind of self-worth. They need to be adored, and of course feared, and this is only possible by being in some kind of relationship with others. I have never known anyone with NPD that enjoyed being alone, at least not until much later in life. They need the applause and the fame like the rest of us need love and care. They must have what they want, when they want, how they want, or they will tap into their inner-toddler and throw a tantrum. They need people around them tending to their every desire, bowing down to them, and treating them like royalty, otherwise they will become enraged or petulant. The moment you stop giving a narcissist what they want, they have no more need for you and will replace you immediately.

How many people has Donald Trump fired now? About 10 when this was written. Now depending on the type of narcissist you are dealing with, how they keep you around will vary. The overt narcissists are just bullies. They will scare you into thinking that you have to stay (in the job/relationship), but the covert narcissist will use the tactic of convincing you that they really care about you, which makes it much harder to get away from them. Understand this though: you are only a source of supply. As soon as you decide you can no longer put up with the abusive or neglectful behavior and walk away, they will replace you with someone else who is clueless and will put up with their bad behavior for as long as it takes them to figure it out. Narcissists are like a tire with a hole in it that is never patched; they need to constantly be refilled. That hole is the deep wound of self-hatred. Again, narcissism is not high self-esteem, it is actually extremely low self-esteem. The outward high self-esteem is just an act.

The reality is that just like with all of our psychic wounds, no one can heal them but ourselves, and since those with NPD don't even think they are sick, they will never patch the hole. They will only keep filling it up with the worship energy of other people. They need this supply of energy to survive, and if they ever get into a position where there is no longer anyone around to supply them with that life-energy, they will slowly wither and die. Just as all human beings cannot live without food, narcissists cannot live without the energy supply of other people.

Since they do not change, just as an illness will not heal without treatment, the only thing you can do to stop the abuse is to get away. Unfortunately, many of us will stay in the relationship, try to manage the best we can, and suffer as our lives get worse and worse.

Manage the Relationship

I agree with most clinicians that the only way (so far) to stop experiencing the damaging effects of behavior from a narcissist is to get away from them. Let me say loud and clear, that I am never one to discount miracles, evolution, and change, but so far, the best thing to do is get away. Since most people either will not do it, cannot do it, or take a very long time to make that decision, we will look at what it looks like to stay involved in the relationship while trying to manage it the best you can.

Some people are genuinely intertwined in a way that is almost completely unavoidable without separation causing major losses, such as if you have a child or are in business together. For the most part however, it is a spouse or family member, and we think that ending a relationship with a family member is too extreme. We believe we will be able to just deal with that person with a 'long stick' type of approach. This belief is heavily supported by a value that every culture shares, which is that nothing is more important than family.

This is very often a wonderful approach to life and many people come from wonderful, loving families—but not all of us. Hitler, Caligula, and Ted Bundy were all part of a family. Should their families have 'stuck beside them?' The family value system can be a beautiful part of the human experience, but it can also be the cause of tremendous suffering because many of us were born to really bad people. In fact, this 'family first' value system is probably the reason cults are such a dangerous phenomenon.

I have always been fascinated by cults. I've studied many of them, and the main commonality among those seduced into joining cults is that they really REALLY want to be a part of a family, usually because they come from one that did not meet their needs. I feel badly saying this for those families, because they may think they did the best they could and that they really love their family member in some cases, but I promise you that there is some deep internal need that was not fulfilled for people attracted to cults. The other commonality about cults is that the leader is always a narcissist, like Jim Jones and David Koresh. These narcissists require their member's absolute worship of and submission to them, and have no problem leading large groups of people straight to their death. I watched a movie about college fraternities, and I realized that the same need for family was true for those who endure all kinds of inhumane treatment and dangerous violence during hazing to be allowed to join.

This is also the case for gangs, churches, and many, many different types of organizations. I believe that a primary need for all of us is the need to belong to a family. This makes sense in light of what babies need to survive, so it is a very primordial and basic need. Of all the things I have observed that can be used to control people including sex, food, and money, I believe that the most powerful compulsion is the need for family. Unless the child has severe psychological issues, it usually takes an extreme amount of abuse for a child to reject a parent.

We all have a powerful need for connections with those we love and who have taken care of us. And let's face it, our very survival is often at stake, especially when we are young, so we develop emotional bonds that are very difficult to break. Family is something so sacred to most of us, that the thought of ending a relationship with a family member because of their bad behavior seems absolutely ludicrous. Simply put, children are attached to their caretakers and they will endure a great amount of abuse if the caretaker happens to have an anti-social personality, just like in cults. We just figure out a way to 'be' that will allow us to endure the abuse. This is supported by most of the people around us in that family, and by the fact that being out in the world all alone with no tribe is too scary to consider, so we stay.

How do you deal with someone who is constantly lying, manipulating you with emotions, belittling you, creating and maintaining a constant environment of instability and chaos and sucking the very life blood out of you? Well, first of all, most of us don't even recognize that this is what they are doing. This is sooooo hard! Please don't be too hard on yourself if you feel it has taken you a long time to see it. Narcissists are MASTERS of illusion. Their actions remind me of that saying, 'pissing on you and telling you it's rain.' They can actually make you feel as if they are your most ardent supporter and friend, when all they really turn out to be is your most beautiful enemy. Doesn't the vampire always turn in to this old, ugly, decrepit looking thing once they begin to die? The beautiful youthful image was just an illusion maintained with blood supply—a gorgeous illusion. Their mastery of illusion is supported by the general reaction many of us have to stress, which is to immediately disconnect and find quick ways to deal with it.

The first quick way is to simply ignore it. Ignoring something requires no real action on your part. It is a matter of not responding and not acting on what you are actually feeling. You cannot continually respond to all the barbs and arrows that are slung by a narcissist, because you would not be very productive, so you begin to ignore a lot of it. This means that you must shut down emotionally to some degree. Shutting down emotionally means hearing and seeing things that bother you, and then stuffing your hurt and pain deep down. You don't respond to it, and you continue on as normal. It's a type of pretending that at least maintains a somewhat bearable atmosphere that is riddled with problems.

Second, you will begin to become an expert problem-solver. Many of the things that narcissists do cause a lot of issues with other people, so you will inevitably be putting out fires. You will have to very often come to the rescue or fix major dilemmas, and this will make you very resourceful. You will become a great conflict manager, analyzer, or negotiator. Managing a relationship with a narcissist will actually give you very viable skill-sets and this can complicate things because it can appear that you are really becoming a very strong person. You will become genuinely skilled at diplomacy, pragmatism, and emotional control.

Third, you will eventually have to rise to the emotional degrees that the narcissist operates at to try to limit the damage that they do. If they yell a lot, you will eventually have to yell back. If they do things behind your back that cause problems, you will begin to put measures in place to minimize the damage. If they are critical and judgmental, you will probably sub-consciously begin to operate in that way in your response to them. Basically, your senses become highly attuned to danger, and you operate in a way that is focused on fixing and/or preventing problems. You go into serious offense mode. You will become a control freak. Since narcissists blame everyone else for all their problems, they often convince you that YOU are the problem, so you will also be constantly trying to fix yourself. It is a constant state of high awareness, mixed with intense numbness and emotional changeability.

Are you starting to get the picture of how crazy it can make you to be in relationship with a narcissist? It is exhausting. It also does not go on forever in the same way; every toxic thing has a cumulative effect, and this is true for dealing with narcissists as well. You can dump toxic waste on a site for years with no outcomes, but eventually those dangerous substances will surface and cause great damage to anything or anyone that is nearby.

As I mentioned earlier, you are prone to losing a lot when in close relationship with narcissists. I have rarely known a person with NPD who didn't have a rack of damaged people around them. Somehow they are always surrounded by people with serious health or life problems. Their children are usually struggling with substance abuse, mental, or physical illnesses, their spouses may have health problems, issues with addiction, or financial difficulties, and they often have friends who have some array of difficult life concerns. The narcissist appears to be the lone warrior in the middle of all these people, often giving the impression that they are supporting or helping them. Women who stay married to a narcissist often struggle with eating disorders, weight issues and depression. Men who stay married to a narcissist struggle with alcohol addiction, anxiety, and heart problems. Children who remain in relationship with a narcissist parent often suffer from long-term health problems, substance abuse, difficulty in relationships, and/or depression. I have personally observed these patterns in the lives of narcissists over the years after having lived in 7 cities, gone to

10 different schools, and lived in over 15 different domiciles. I've known a lot of them! I've known a lot of people whose parents are narcissists. I have watched the damage they cause play out over decades.

Being in business with a narcissist is almost a guarantee that you will lose a great deal over the years. I have seen people lose large amounts of money, a business, their home, and their good health. Yet, even after tremendous loss, we will stay by their side because we cannot imagine that it is at all ok to just leave. I have often noticed as well, that the narcissist keeps people hanging on with the promise of some prize at the end of it all that will make all your sacrifice worth it. The covert narcissists are also very good at pretending to want to change because they know that will keep you in relationship with them and that is truly the main thing they want because they cannot live without someone to abuse. Doling out abuse is almost as necessary to the narcissist as breathing is for the rest of us.

But the main thing I have observed, is that they are able to keep the people around them enduring the abuse because many of us are compassionate, caring, loving, patient, tolerant people who genuinely want to help others, and we think that this person we love who continues to lead us down the road to annihilation just needs HELP. We just need to help them to see the truth, recover from the illness, understand their behavior, change their habits, or learn something they don't know that will alter their conduct. If they just understood how their trauma and/or abuse has affected them; if they could just see how much they are hurting you; if they are just able to heal from their pain, they will change. You will wind up giving them so much help, that you give everything you have and your life is destroyed.

What happens to you?

How is your life destroyed? Addiction, depression, anxiety, illness, financial loss, failed relationships, destruction of business or career, and complete loss of self-esteem are the main culprits. This is particularly true if the narcissist is a parent. A parent holds the responsibility for a child's ego development and under the conditions stated, you can end up with a seriously damaged ego, and this will make it very challenging for you to recognize, achieve, and maintain a joyful life. Your senses have basically been attuned to how to handle an abusive person, so you don't even recognize or know what to do with a healthy person or situation. You are so used to being lied to, manipulated and/or controlled, that you never trust anyone's seemingly kind behavior. You have been let down, used, under-valued, and disrespected so many times, it is what is most familiar to you and as mentioned before, we tend to be attracted to what is familiar. The familiar is comfortable. Comfortable feels secure. This is true for food and people.

I remember the moment I realized that I was actually turned on by chaos and suffering. I was on the phone with a lover who was in a great deal of turmoil over his own narcissistic mother, and I suddenly became very aroused and wanted to go have sex with him. For the first time in my life (this was in my 40's), I consciously asked myself, why am I sexually turned on by someone who is in a state of distress? I Googled it. Sure enough, articles appeared about how child-hood abuse leads to attractions to people and situations that mirror those feelings you had as a child. What a moment of clarity this was for me! We so seldom actually question our attractions and desires. Why do I like people who look like this, or act like that? Why am I always in similar relationship situations? For the most part we just operate on automatic, never considering that much of who we think we are, or what we want, has been conditioned by circumstances that we have been in.

Conditioning is a powerful thing—POWERFUL I tell you! Behavior can be altered or created by conditioning. This is easy to see with animals, but it is also true for humans. Undoing that conditioning is so challenging, because most of us don't even recognize our conditioning. Since family conditioning occurs in the most formative years of your brain, physical, and ego development, it is the most compelling and can lead to the most permanent damage. Long after the dependent state of being a child is over, we continue to put ourselves in damaging situations because we don't realize that the main thing we are attracted to, is healing from trauma. Who doesn't want to heal? We may not know it consciously, but so much of our lives are our attempts at healing from trauma.

Healing from Trauma

How does one heal from trauma? Well, there are a variety of ways, but I would say that the most important thing to understand is that it is a process. It is rare that anyone experiences sudden, quick, permanent recovery from any ailment. Healing usually requires a series of steps. The most pertinent step though, is to actually get OUT of the harmful situation.

Can you heal from the effects of say, lead poisoning if you continue to be exposed to the lead? Can you heal from lung cancer if you continue to smoke cigarettes? Can you heal from obesity if you continue to over-eat? There is nothing you can heal from if you don't initially remove your exposure to whatever caused your problem in the first place. You cannot heal from a toxic relationship if you stay in the relationship. This is at the least, the very first step you must take. The cold truth is that you have so much more work to do following that step to actually heal, but this is a required step.

Further healing from any malady requires medicine, therapy, recovery time, and avoidance of whatever brought on the problem, but none of those things will work if you return to that thing that caused the problem.

It is a very difficult lesson to learn in the case of relationships with narcissists, because they have figured out in their zeal to control everything in their lives, exactly what you like, what you need, and how much to give you to keep you around them. It could be food if they are a good cook, money if they have lots of it, gifts, a job, a house, or any other thing that is needed to function. Most people will simply stay in the relationship, and either catch the narcissist virus, or slowly deteriorate under the weight of extremely dysfunctional circumstances. This eventually destroys your ability to have empathy for others because it is difficult to say the least, to sympathize with other people's pain when you are working 24/7 to carry your own.

After years of responding and relating to the narcissist, you will lose your ability to relate healthily to anyone. Anything that is done repeatedly will eventually become habitual. This is what conditioning actually is. It's just repetition! It really is very simple—repeated stimuli that eventually creates a habitual response. You hit a dog on the nose enough times after it poops on the floor and it will stop pooping on the floor. You constantly question and point out the flaws in someone's thoughts or behavior and they will eventually lose confidence in themselves. You have dinner ready at 7 pm every night and everyone will stop what they are doing at 7 to come to the table. You lie to someone enough times and they will eventually lose the ability to trust you. If you feel bad every day for 18 years, you will most likely continue to feel bad until you are able to go back and root out what made you feel bad in the first place. Human beings are at the same time resilient and fragile creatures. I think because we have seen so many examples of our ability to survive after war, torture, abuse, etc., we tend to focus on our resilience. It's true, we can survive anything, but what it turns us into is what makes us so fragile.

Because of the deleterious effects of conditioning due to exposure to repetitive and stressful stimuli, the first step to healing from the trauma this causes is to get out of those stressful circumstances.

What else can you do?

Before we get into some of the other things you can do to start the healing process, I do want to point out another aspect of human fragility that narcissists capitalize on. I mentioned earlier how they figure out the things you like or need and give it to you to keep you around, and how those things mainly fall into the category of material or external things like support or gifts. There is one other thing that narcissists truly understand is absolutely irresistible to most human beings, and that is LOVE. Most of those things we mentioned are at their essence, expressions of love, and this need for love that every single human being has is at the core of how narcissists keep you around.

This word love … we certainly use it a lot. There are so many forms of it, degrees of it, expressions of it, and definitions of it. There is no doubt however, that all human beings need it. Apparently even plants need it. Because this is such an obvious need that we have, it is also obvious to narcissists, and they will figure out how to convince the people they are connected to that they genuinely love them. For so many of us, this is not a difficult task. People associate very simple things with love. These include being fed, being clothed and housed, given the things you need, and sometimes just being talked to. I would say though, that a significant sign of love for many of us is the idea of being NEEDED. When someone constantly needs your assistance, your help, your presence, or your input, it makes you feel needed, which makes you feel valued, which makes you feel loved. The fact that this is combined with abuse and neglect does not seem to diminish the certainty people have that they are indeed loved by the narcissist.

It is a tricky discussion to have, but I am of the notion that narcissists don't truly know how to love. In my opinion, true love is when you want what is best for the person you care for—best for their development, health, success, and well-being. This is even the case if whatever is best for them may be something that causes you discomfort or inconvenience.

This is simply not true for those with NPD. Anything that causes them discomfort or inconvenience is vehemently avoided, even in circumstances where someone they supposedly love is in harm's way. Unfortunately, since most of us have been raised with the notion that corporeal punishment is acceptable, there is also an automatic mass acceptance that a bit of intentionally inflicted pain goes hand in hand with love. This makes it quite challenging to properly judge just how much that bit should be before you might actually not be loved by someone. I am of the mind that at this point, we need to start promoting the concept that even if someone does genuinely love you, it is still not acceptable for them to inflict pain on you—verbally, physically, or emotionally. Anyway, sometimes the only way to see your own situation with some clarity, is to seek out information from outside sources. This is why films and literature are so invaluable. Hearing other people's stories can help you to see your own story in a more objective light.

So, other things you can do #1 is: Watch and read biographies and autobiographies! I definitely have a list of favorite movies and documentaries that helped me to put my experience in perspective. There are many movies that are about characters with NPD (though it might not always be explicitly stated) and how destructive they are. One of my favorites is *August: Osage County* (2013) staring the great Meryl Streep. Her leading character is the narcissistic mother of a family of people who are all severely damaged, and she is the reason why. *Mommie Dearest* (1981), as I've mentioned, is another classic, detailing the life of the famous actress Joan Crawford from the point of view of her daughter Christina. Now, thanks to Netflix and Amazon Prime, there are numerous documentaries about infamous narcissists including Ted Bundy, Jeffrey Epstein, and that Tiger King dude, not one of whom came to a good end. I have included a list of other movies and documentaries at the end of this book to watch that I think are great examples of narcissistic personalities and the abuse they heap on those around them. When you see the behavior displayed by other narcissists, it helps you to identify what you have been going through.

Thing #2: Talk

It is challenging for us to be able to see what is wrong with our lives when our situation is all we know. Whatever is happening in our homes is what is normal to us and what shapes us, despite what we may witness or experience in the outside world. Our thinking, expectations, boundaries, and behavior are all shaped by the treatment of our caretakers, and even when it has not been the best treatment, for us, it is what we recognize as love. This is distorted even more by a global cultural value of keeping personal things private. We are all taught to keep our mouths shut about what is going on at home and in our personal lives, and many people feel a great deal of shame about their abuse, thinking that no one else is having this experience. Secrecy is a very tricky thing; it can protect the vulnerable as well as the predator.

Now don't get me wrong, I am baffled at the new culture of reality TV and how willing everyone is to share all their drama with the world. I guess I am a bit old-school and definitely agree with the notion that you should keep most of your private business to yourself. We are all learning, growing, and making mistakes. You don't want all of that to be in the public eye, and I am sure many entertainers whole-heartedly agree with that. In my opinion the Paparazzi people are truly despicable human beings. But sometimes keeping things secret is very dangerous.

With all of the negative aspects that technology and this 'information age' that we are in has presented, including the pollution created from mining for the parts needed for these gadgets, and the emotional and physical stress that the electricity from these devices cause, one of the more positive outcomes of this 'information age' we are presently in is a greater awareness of the vast amount of suffering people have experienced and are suffering behind closed doors. This has provided increased means for their escape, and retribution for their perpetrators. However, even with all the transparency that seems to exist now, things like sex trafficking and pedophilia still persist, and this is because what is not seen can continue. Again, whatever you know is what is normal to you, and it generally does not cross a child's mind to tell others what is happening in their home. In many cases, children are explicitly told not to tell with the fear of punishment or even death held over them.

So, the #2 other thing to do if you even slightly feel that you have been abused, is to talk to someone about it—maybe even a few someone's! This is also very true for romantic relationships, which tend to fall under the scrutiny of intense secrecy, particularly because sex is involved.

It is highly recommended that if you are suffering in any kind of relationship, seek to find out as much as you can about other people's relationships so you have something to compare to. ASK QUESTIONS. Asking questions like, has anyone else experienced what I am experiencing?, have a lot of people experienced what I am experiencing?, how have they responded to it?, and is there any information to help me understand what I am feeling? is so incredibly important. These are all very important questions.

You are a human being worthy of kindness and respect. You deserve happiness. You deserve to be loved. If you feel you are not getting these things, ask questions, do research, and talk to people. Find out if it is you, or if it is that you are being abused by someone you think loves you. One of the most dangerous weapons that narcissists use is the silence that everyone upholds on the details of their relationship with that narcissist, so that no one is aware of just how destructive this person is to EVERYONE. And destructive they are. I have seen countless instances where one person is abusing multiple people and none of them know because no one is talking.

It is very difficult to get people to talk about the things that hurt them. I say that as someone who falls into that category. For me, this was exacerbated because one of the things my mother used to do was use information against me. Any moment of vulnerability I shared with her, such as being afraid of failing a test or feeling insecure about a high school performance, was always brought up at another time when she was angry with me to point to some character deficiency I possessed such as insecurity or fear. I quickly learned to keep things to myself, and definitely assumed that was something I should do with everyone all the time in order to protect myself. I said nothing about what I was going through as a child.

It took me a long time to begin to talk to people, share my stories and my feelings, and be honest and vulnerable. Once I did, I quickly learned that I was not only not to blame for my suffering, but also not alone in it. Talk about the experiences you are having with that abusive person in your life with someone you trust. Tell the other people in your family so you all can compare stories. This 'don't talk about people' shyte is one of the major ways that narcissists thrive. CALL THEM OUT. There are so many people who are victims of narcissists. Because well, you know, it's an epidemic.

No Contact

I just can't say it enough times. It may not be possible for it to be permanent in every case, so sometimes it can simply at least be for a period of time, like say if the narcissist is the parent of your child, but a key part of recovering from narcissistic abuse is getting away from the narcissist. In the NPD discussion forums we call it 'No contact.' You cannot truly begin the healing process until you are no longer interacting with them.

I mentioned earlier how you cannot heal from lead poisoning until you get away from the lead, and this is true of anything toxic. Narcissist are truly toxic human beings. They poison and destroy everyone and everything around them. They are walking containers of destruction; they cannot help it.

Every way they are, think, and behave ultimately ends up in the destruction of something. This is why there are so many of them in some of the jobs that attract sociopaths. Many of those career choices (lawyer/cop/social worker) are all in the position of determining someone's fate, and narcissists absolutely excel at that. So, the only way to stop the destruction of your life is to remove yourself from the circumstances that are causing that destruction.

Going silent with the narcissist is also a very good measuring tool, because when you stop talking to someone, they will show you who they are. I have seen this so many times. A healthy person will express sadness over the disconnection, and then leave you alone. Not a narcissist. Over time, they will slowly break down when you ignore them. I will never forget what happened back in the 90's when I had one of those first answering machines. I had stopped talking to my mom for about 2 weeks, and over the course of a week, her messages went from "I am just worried about you sweetie, please call me" to her yelling and screaming into the machine how selfish and self-centered I was in shrieking tones. I have also witnessed it with a good friend who stopped talking to his narcissistic mentor after having received several insane messages from him as a result of not responding to an initial call within 24 hours. In the end, he had sent my friend over 45 text messages and voicemails railing into him about what a horrible person he was, all because of what he felt was not a timely enough response to an initial call ... whew.

Since every way that narcissist's think, talk, and relate has a dose of toxicity in it, by relating and responding to them, you are constantly taking in and responding to toxicity. You are communicating with someone who is always secretly just trying to get their way. Nothing is ever actually what it is about. When you respond in the normal, healthy way that most human beings respond to the daily interactions we have with one another requiring empathy and consideration, you are met with veiled criticisms, often hidden in jokes or off-the-cuff remarks, or outright rage and tantrums so that you are consistently in a state of defense, offense, fixing, and various forms of pleading for understanding. The reality is that you don't even know who you are outside of responding to stressful situations.

Ask yourself, what kind of person would I be if I were happy, doing things I love, around people who supported and believed in me, and/or pursuing my goals? Instead we stay. We stay out of values of loyalty, family, love, support, and religious or spiritual beliefs. We stay until we almost have no other choice but to let go, and by that time we are usually bereft, broke, and suffering from poor health, depression, and a complete loss of identity. Please, get away. Trust that if you are wrong, and the person really does love you, that will be revealed. Be willing to make a mistake. Be willing to discover that you are stronger than you think. Be willing to let go of a painful life.

Chapter 6

FINAL THOUGHTS

"It is no measure of good health to be well adjusted to a sick society." - Krishnamurti

Healing

The most ideal outcome of being in a relationship with a narcissist, is to not only get out of it, but to heal from it. This can take a lifetime, so please be patient with yourself and others. The damage that narcissists cause can be so deep and so far-reaching, that it can seem as if you will never completely get over it. I have very often felt that way.

Long-term effects of my mother's abuse of me crop up all the time, even though I feel as if I have finally been able to forgive her. I genuinely no longer think of her with anguish on a daily basis, and I truly understand that she was also abused into what she became. As suggested in this book, I believe she was part of a legacy in this culture whose history has nurtured the proliferation of mental illness and narcissism through systemic mistreatment of human beings, and like her, I believe most of them are not at all aware of what they have become.

When I see old black and white pictures from lynching's or footage from today of the leering faces of racist white people in a gathering like the one that occurred recently in D.C. prior to the assault on the U.S. Capitol, there is always such an intensely oblivious sense of righteousness and justification in their eyes. They clearly believe to the core of their beings that they are correct and rational. There is no sense that they are aware at all of the pain and suffering felt by generations of people of color in this country. I also never saw any indication in my mother's eyes until her death that she was aware of the pain she was causing me.

I deeply believe in understanding that most of the ways people mistreat you have nothing what-so-ever to do with your inadequacies—only theirs. I promise you that abusive people were ALWAYS abused themselves. My mother's mother was very abusive towards her. According to my mom, she was an alcoholic, had been a prostitute, and had been gang raped at the age of 14. When she died, she was so obese that the EMT's had to double up two gurneys to get her body out of her apartment, which she probably had not left in almost 20 years. When I would visit my family in California for the summer as a child, my paternal grandmother would take me to visit her, and she would just sit in a chair at a table in her small one-bedroom apartment in a senior living facility in San Francisco, drink whiskey, and watch soap-opera's. Sheesh I hated the smell in there! It was a rotting, putrid, dusty aroma of impending death. I remember my mother telling me once that she asked her mother for any baby pictures of her and her mother replied, "You were too ugly."

Her mother had five children that the state took away years before my mother and her sister were born. The story has major holes in it, but apparently, she went to the courts because her husband was beating her and taking her money, and her children were taken away and parceled out for adoption. My mother located a few of them when I was 16 and it was crazy because they looked just like her mother! So yeah, I have a whole host of family out there I know nothing about. One of the most heart-breaking moments I have ever experienced in my life is when my mother told me that when she went to San Francisco to clear out her mother's apartment after she died, she found the hospital baby-bracelets for all five of those children tucked carefully away in a trunk underneath her bed. My goodness . . . the sorrows that people have.

It took so many years for me to find out all the details of my mother's life that helped me to understand who she was. Like the fact that she got an STD the very first time she ever had sex, or how her stepfather used to hit her on the head with a fork at dinner, or how the first child she ever took care of, which was her sister's baby, had died at 7 yrs. old, or how she became a Mormon because they were so poor living in the projects of Potrero Hill. The missionaries came to her door and told her they would give them a bag of groceries every week if she joined the church, and then when it was time to go on the Mission, they would not allow her to go because they found out she was Black. Up to that point she had been the most devout member of the congregation, often testifying behind the pulpit in church. Needless to say, that destroyed her belief in God, and she was never spiritually inclined again until close to her death.

Ironically, all five of my mother's sister's children suffered difficult fates as well. The little girl that died at 7 years old had the 'brittle bone' disease Osteogenesis imperfecta, and her bones were always breaking as a baby; another was beaten to death by a cocaine-addled boyfriend in a 2 am drug-rage while asleep in his crib, the other sister witnessed this horrific act, went into a catatonic state, and was taken away from her mother (my aunt) in a horrible type of repetitive generational irony. I later found out that she was molested in one of the foster homes where she was sent. My aunt's oldest daughter, and the only cousin that I had even had any contact with, died of a heart-attack a few years ago. She wasn't even 50.

Generations of suffering are my family legacy. This is true for so many. This is true for absolutely every person of color I know. Our families are riddled with addiction and illness. In a twisted continuing cycle of the legacy of African families separated on auction blocks and Indigenous families pushed onto reservations, we have subconsciously continued our own self-destruction in response to relentless oppression. Crack really put the nail in that coffin! But we have continued on, kept together the best we could, and tried to make the best of a tough situation.

I have a lot of compassion for my mother now, and I am even able to be thankful for some of the gifts she gave me. She was so incredibly brilliant and so passionate about helping to change this world. Her students loved her so much. She was also hysterically funny—she had me in stitches all the time. One of the things I appreciated most about her was that she didn't put on any airs and was very down-to-earth. I always felt like I could be myself around her. This made it agonizing to realize that I could not be in a relationship with her.

It is beyond confusing to understand and accept the duality in human beings; that someone can be both wonderful and hellfire at the same damn time. I have noticed that many, many people choose to ignore the abuse that has been doled out to them by people they love, mainly because they feel so much compassion for them. You can find this narrative illustrated in many a story about domestic abuse from men, but you don't see it as much in stories about family. They choose to just cast the abusive kin in a particular narrative, usually one of the suffering martyr, because it is just too painful for them to admit and deal with the fact that someone they really loved and needed treated them awfully. We saw how Ike abused Tina in *What's Love Got to Do With It?* (1993), but we did not see how her mother abused her.

I believe this is particularly difficult for Black men who had/have a narcissistic mother. Just like with the so-called 'daddy issues' that women have, sons are really geared towards protecting and cherishing their mothers, and the racial component of the suffering that so many Black women have endured in this country makes it so hard for them to see their mother as anything but a victim. That is always how I saw my mother. The truth is that she was a very damaged person, like so many of us that are victims of this incredibly dysfunctional cultural system.

She passed away from cancer in 2011, and I am so thankful that I went to her side during her illness because somehow, in her last days, she got a glimpse of the truth of who she had been and what she had done, and we really connected in a very heart-felt way. In the last years of her life, she really made an effort to heal and to face her darkness. She had begun to investigate spiritual practices like Yoga and meditation, she went out of her way to take care of her finances so that she could leave me and my sister money, but most importantly, she absolutely adored my daughter. Though she could never quite completely destroy that narcissism disease that she had been infected with for so long, I truly believe that she tried to make things right with me before she passed away. I will never forget sitting beside her in the bed after she came home for hospice, watching her brain slowly deteriorate as the tumors spread. She began to yell out random things like, "I have a meeting at 2!" She could barely speak, and she kept looking up at the fan and squeezing my hand. I asked her, "Mom are you cold?" She blinked her eyes really slowly and so I got up and turned the fan off. When I came back and took her hand, to my surprise she said clearly, "You are the most caring person I know." I just cried … She said things to me I never thought I would hear from her, and I took every word into my heart and into my soul, and I was able to forgive her. It was such a relief, and I am so grateful that I had that opportunity.

This was not the same person who sat in a restaurant with me and my father the first time we visited him when I was 16, and very callously told him to his great shock and dismay, that his mother had tried to commit suicide after he had hijacked the airplane. I will never forget the look on his face … just utter anguish.

She did not pass easily—it was a very difficult death, and I understood why. The irony of someone dying from colo-rectal cancer who had been vegan most of their life was not lost on me. I remember thinking of a quote I had heard once: "It is more important what comes out of your mouth than what goes into it." It was quite affirming for me as well, because I saw the fruits of unkindness, and I felt relieved and empowered that I had chosen to take another path—or at least I have certainly tried my best! I am quite sure with all my own imperfections I have caused some harm along the way, but I am absolutely committed to ending the cycles in my lineage and I see the evidence of that in my own daughter who is so kind and so healthy. She does not do drugs, she takes care of herself, and she has really healthy self-esteem.

But I am still trying to fix problems with my teeth because my mother never took me to the dentist. I still have sciatica pain from time to time because of that uneven parallel-bars accident for which I never received any treatment. I feel as if I am finally conquering depression after almost 50 years, but the suicidal thoughts I have had for decades sometimes linger in the back of my consciousness like a distant song.

The main long-term effect however, is the constant fear and self-doubt that accompanies being in any kind of relationship. It took me 50 years to realize that I am extremely afraid of getting close to women. I always think a lover will abandon me eventually. And really, the bottom line is that I am deeply co-dependent, and always attracted to very broken people because I have been so broken myself. There is always this little voice inside my brain whispering things to me about loss, betrayal, and endings. It is so incredibly challenging to change your life by training your brain into a state where you are having different thoughts, which leads to different feelings, and different behaviors. With significant injuries, there is often a scar that never completely fades, and this is the case with relationship abuse. The scars are not made of tissue, but of thoughts, feelings, habits, and fears. Narcissistic abuse is a trauma whose effects linger long after the abuse is over, just like with PTSD, and it most assuredly takes time, effort, and patience to recover. This has been true for me and every person that I know who has experienced NPD abuse.

I struggle with the fact that I don't necessarily think talk-therapy is completely effective in healing from abuse. I have always tried to be diplomatic when discussing this, especially since I actually have a Master's in Psychology. I was watching a special on PBS recently about the high levels of trauma in children in the U.S., and a woman speaking about her own childhood trauma admitted that she had been in talk-therapy for a decade, that it did not work, and she wasn't able to find any real relief until she tried alternative methods of healing. This made me feel better about my opinion. I have heard this many times from long-term talk-therapy patients.

A large part of my resistance is also the fact that I have experienced quite a few very unethical, and honestly, sometimes just plain un-intelligent people in the medical field during my 25+ years battle with poor health, and I would assume that the same is the case for mental illness professionals. I have encountered a large number of doctors that simply did not give a shit. Doctors reflect the same multi-dimensionality that humans possess anywhere—some are good at what they do, some are not. Don't get bullied into thinking that just because someone has the label of 'Dr.' it automatically means they are a true healer. Take your time picking a therapist, listen to your gut if it doesn't feel right, and don't be afraid to try a different person. I do think talk-therapy is effective in un-covering the reasons for your suffering, but healing from that suffering is quite another thing.

What does healing actually encompass? What does it mean to heal from something? Well, physically, a wound must close, new skin must form, new tissue and cells generated, and inflammation and infection must be cleared. We also tend to be more careful and aware about the thing that is responsible for our injury, such as driving too fast if you are hurt in a car accident, or drinking too much alcohol if you have liver disease, so we will also probably change some behavior. Healing is a multi-faceted, multi-dimensional journey, and I don't believe just talking will get you to the finish line. And look, I am aware of cognitive-behavioral therapy and the many methods that those who use talk-therapy employ to provoke behavioral changes, but my feeling is that if it took years and years of inter-relating to create dysfunction, it will take some mighty powerful external influences to un-do the damage caused. Since we are multi-faceted as emotional, mental, and physical beings, it will take multi-faceted techniques to bring all those elements back into balance.

Psychiatry has recently begun to employ well-being practices from other cultures, integrating them into allopathic treatments for mental and physical ailments. Examples are the use of plant medicines and meditation. Many of these 'alternative' methods originally may have had nothing to do with treatment of an ailment, but were only a part of a healthy lifestyle. We are now all familiar with the term alternative medicine, but let me clarify that what this term often encompasses are techniques from other cultures that simply promote well-being. This includes Chinese Daoist practices, Indian Ayurvedic and spiritual practices, and many other Indigenous methods of care.

In order to truly heal, it is important to understand that everything that happens in the mind happens in the body, and you cannot truly heal if you attend to one and not the other. Therefore, it is important not only to talk, to think, to consider, and to discover, but also to breathe, sweat, drink and eat healthy foods, and engage in practices that balance the mind and the body to eliminate physical AND psychological toxins. I can testify that the most relief I have experienced has been from alternative methods of healing. More and more health practitioners are beginning to embrace these alternative techniques for healing, but you have to have the money, status, or knowledge to get to them, and that is not always easy for the average person. It certainly was not for me; I was caught in the vicious cycle of being in too much pain to work, so not having health insurance, having to work in pain, and thus exacerbating my illnesses. Most health insurance plans do not cover many of these alternative methodologies anyway, so the bottom line is that the main thing you need is money.

What this means is that the people who are the most vulnerable to abuse, also have the least access to treatment. Remember, the predator doesn't go after the cub that is surrounded by strong lionesses who are protecting it, they go after the abandoned, small, weak prey because it is much easier to capture. Don't get eaten! And if you have had a few bites taken out of you, please make it your priority in life to heal those wounds. This is especially valid considering almost every predator was once prey. Wounds can either lead to understanding and strength, or compliance and imitation. Be unique. Be better than your predator. Acknowledge your illness. Get treatment. Forgive. Heal.

What happens to the narcissists?

A very good friend of mine said something so hilarious and so poignant as he was casually observing his narcissistic mother. He said, "She needs a t-shirt that says, 'does not play well with others." He pretty much encapsulated half of this book in a very simple statement! The final outcome for narcissists however, is not quite so light-hearted.

This is the part where I tell you that you that they do not get away with what they have done to you. They aren't simply left in the sandbox to sulk because they kept hitting the other kids with their toys. What usually winds up happening is, well, something akin to the fates of narcissists like Robert Durst and Harvey Weinstein. Their lives usually end with their own slow, painful demise, and/or a legacy of evil that erases any good they did while living, like with Bill Cosby (I personally know women who interacted with him and I definitely believe all 52 of those women are telling the truth).

What is interesting to me is that ultimately, narcissism is a death of the spirit, making ego the master, who then proceeds to put on a life-long show, much like many of the narcissists mentioned. This is always a response to not having needs met at a crucial time in development, combined with significant abuse during that time, and simultaneously being allowed certain privileges. Again, the formula for narcissism is privilege and abuse. The narcissist learned that they must perform, trick, and manipulate to get their needs met. The needs that were not being met include acknowledgment, value, worth, and connectedness.

Every child goes through a period of "look at me!" They want their caregiver to see what they can do—that they are capable. This acknowledgement of capability makes us feel good about ourselves, and we feel able to contribute something of ourselves. That ability to contribute gives us worth and value in our community. It gives our life meaning. This is what everyone wants—a life that has meaning. This is why Indigenous cultures prioritize ceremonies and rites of passage. The important thing to understand is that when someone will do anything to achieve that acknowledgment of worth and value, it's because they never actually got it as a child, and they are now obsessed with constantly getting it as an adult in the only ways that they understand will bring it to them. Whatever this is, was taught to you by your caregivers.

For Donald Trump (and really, almost all narcissists), it is making money. In fact, he himself claimed he had a brother who drank himself to death because he was not as concerned with making money like the rest of the family; apparently he mainly wanted to fly airplanes and sail boats, but this was not valued in his family, so he numbed himself to the pain he felt of having no worth or value with alcohol, and basically drank himself to death[1].

Whatever the 'thing' is, is usually something that gives you a good measure of freedom or power—beauty, money, skill, status—they allow you the opportunity to do what you want when you want, and listen, narcissists will do do do do do them to death!

Another favorite scene of mine on the outcome for narcissists is from *The Sopranos* (1999) in Season 2, Episode 11 'House Arrest' when Dr. Melfi is explaining a disorder that most narcissists have to Tony Soprano. She explains: "Alyxathymia is a psychological disorder common in certain personalities where the individual craves almost ceaseless action which enables them to avoid acknowledging the abhorrent things they do." Tony asks what happens when they stop, and she answers, "They have time to think about their behavior, how what they do affects other people, about feelings of emptiness and self-loathing haunting them since childhood, and they crash."

What did she mean by crash? A perfect example of this is anti-communist, anti-Gay, McCarthy-era lawyer Roy Cohn, who in a lyrical irony was himself Gay. He worked for the Mafia and Donald Trump, partied and worked hard every day of his life, and then suddenly dropped dead at 59 from the self-destructive stress of a corrupt career. For some, life can even stretch into their 70's, but either way the crash, or death, is quite dramatic. Cohn died of AIDS after being disbarred for unethical conduct.

I have seen it time and again. Narcissists do not have gentle deaths surrounded by loved ones. There is usually a lot of physical suffering, battling over inheritance, and the stress of watching what was once an extremely capable person turn into a helpless child. They will also exhibit all the rage that comes with losing one's autonomy and abilities as the bad-ass they have always been.

Utilizing the history of the mafia in the U.S. for *The Sopranos* (1999) was definitely a poetic example of how culture contributes to certain pathologies, and specifically how the murderous, violent foundation of that crew obviously created numerous psychopaths, sociopaths, and narcissists. One of the things I have always noticed about those with NPD, is that even when there is no NPD diagnosis (and this is true most of the time; this is something that is just very difficult for psychiatrists to identify without extensive time spent with a patient), there is often a long list of other mental health diagnoses. This includes some type of substance addiction, PTSD, Bi-polar disorder, depression, anxiety, and borderline personality. These diagnoses of what was a significantly successful and accomplished person can be quite surprising to their family members.

I must say I find it quite interesting that the U.S. is plagued with the highest numbers of diseases like cancer, diabetes, addiction, and mental illness … meanwhile we portray this image of diversity, opportunity, freedom, and prosperity …

The achievement and success that narcissists are obsessed with is really just another addiction, and all addiction is about avoidance of pain. People drink too much alcohol or shoot heroin because they are in extreme emotional pain. It is unfortunate that so many of us look at addiction as a personal fault. Because admitting 'faults' can be so painful, particularly for those with NPD, narcissists will never EVER admit to their weaknesses or to what they are, and they become addicted to enhancing their self-image. Another great definition of NPD that I found was in an article by Jacob Davaney in an online magazine called *Collective Evolution* which stated that narcissism is "self-absorption to the extent that it will adopt any set of rationale to protect the ego which often includes a degree of self-deception[2]." With NPD, there is an enormous addiction to self-deception. This is probably why narcissism is just as much of an epidemic as opioids—it is actually just another pain treatment. They are self-medicating the pain of trauma with accomplishments. It is much more dangerous however, because no one will deny that Fentanyl is dangerous, but who the hell is claiming that ambition is dangerous?

The narrative that is given to us regarding money and success is a lot of propaganda. If you take the time to really look into their lives, rich, successful people are often no happier than the rest of us. We are certainly fed enough images to convince us that life is great when you are rich and that all of the wonderful things you acquire will bring you a sense of satisfaction, but it just isn't true, and you can find many a film, book, documentary, or testimony from a rich person to verify this[3].

The truth is, narcissism often leads to a very bad end. This includes illness, loneliness, loss, depression, and an agonizing death. Is it worth it to die in a million-dollar room, all alone? Is it worth it to have seven heart surgeries like Dick Cheney? To end your life in prison half-blind like Bill Cosby? Shuffled around to multiple court cases in your 80's like Harvey Weinstein? Let me say this loud and clear: The people around a narcissist suffer, but so does the narcissist. This concept of connection, and that what you put out you get back is the truth. It may take a while, but what goes around does indeed come around. It may appear that evil people get away with evil, but if you look closely and do the research, that is not always true, and this is the narrative that we need to start promoting much more than we presently do.

There really has been an historical cover-up when it comes to the fates of destructive abusive people. I invite all my readers to really look into powerful people's lives. Pay attention to all of these movies that are made about them. Watch documentaries and shows like *Drunk History* (2013). Really think about things like heart disease and strokes, and what it feels like to exist in a state of debilitating health for years at a time. The narcissists wind up suffering some of the same things that their victims do, and all the champagne and diamonds in the world cannot make up for poor health and physical suffering.

I mentioned earlier that a lot of horror movies are based on true stories. We look at them as these exaggerated works of fiction, but human beings have done horrific things over the centuries, and most of those human beings have come to a terrible end. Read about Kings and Queens, Generals of war, retired cops, wealthy CEO's of pharmaceutical companies. I could give you many more examples than I have, but I promise you it does not tend to end well. Unfortunately, we have been so brain-washed into believing that success and money bring a great deal of satisfaction, that it is hard for us to really fathom the level of pain that many who have achieved a certain level of success experience at the end of their lives. It seems inconsequential compared to every victory they won prior to a slow laborious death, like with George Bush, but until you have experienced a slow laborious death, you cannot appreciate the sheer horror of it. Robert Durst, the Baekelands, O.J. Simpson, and Jose Menendez were all very wealthy. It did not end well for them.

Do you know how one of the founders of Baskin-Robbins died? Do you know how the founder of McDonalds, famous seller of carcinogenic food died? Do you know how many of oil tycoon J. Paul Getty's children died? Because we do know how those of us who have consumed their products are doing—not well. We are full of diabetes and heart disease because of fast food, and our oceans are utterly polluted and toxic because of oil companies. Furthermore, the social impact of the legacies of narcissists is extensive. Would there even be an opioid epidemic without the Sackler family[4]?

It may be that it is not just helpful to understand narcissism, but essential if we want to save ourselves. We are certainly experiencing enough violence, poverty, illness, and depression to warrant a serious look at the people who are making the decisions that shape our world today. Because while their victims seek help, narcissists do not. The tremendous volume of grief caused by the behaviors of narcissists is over-whelming, and this is evident in our pandemics of addiction, mental illness and disease, and now specifically, narcissism.

Popular culture is obsessed with attractiveness, and you must smile, which often means suppressing your grief, which means disassociation, which means dysfunction. Because of how fame and money oriented we are now, there has developed this 'value' of always being positive and upbeat because it's attractive. Obviously inner joy is genuinely beautiful and inspiring and ultimately what we all strive for when it's real, but now it has become a commodity, and we are just hiding our fear and pain. And really, pain is just another emotion in the whole spectrum of emotions which includes joy, ecstasy, doubt, anger, passion, elation, regret—all of it. I think one of the reasons we love people like Richard Pryor and Robin Williams is their authenticity—they gave you ALL of it.

Now everyone is just bragging and smiling and looking good for the selfie. I have been guilty of it myself. But the truth is that everything has an ebb and flow. It seems more logical to me now that to be in harmony with that flow you have to allow what comes. If you are happy, be happy, but if you are sad, be honest about the fact that you are sad. I truly believe that one of the main reasons there is so much addiction, and why we are having this opioid and narcissism epidemic, is because so many of us are suppressing our grief.

And I mean shit, the world is on FIRE. How can you even be human and not feel some major pain just over the state of the earth? Impossible. War. Everywhere.

The duality is that beautiful and amazing things are also happening like shifts in consciousness and technological advancements, but there has been a lot of loss. Ultimately, the hardest thing to achieve is authenticity—no matter what you are feeling. It doesn't always win you friends. People want to feel better, not worse. Well, the 'worse' part just sits in there and festers until it explodes, or morphs into something really ugly. And hey, you need things to keep that grief at bay, like heroin and pills. And money. But emotions are energy-in-motion, and energy HAS to move, so it will come out, one way or the other.

Finally

"Sweet sweet fate, I've had about all I can take, am I living in a bed that I made ..." - H.E.R., Fate (2019)

The most difficult thing about having been raised by a narcissist is the constant life-long battle with self-destructive habits, and the incredible impact they have on the quality of your life. When I was young, I always thought that forgiving my mother, letting go, and moving on with my life was the most challenging thing for me. Not so. The most challenging thing was the continual heartbreak from failed relationships and friendships that are a result of having a tendency towards making poor choices in friends and acquaintances, or my own confusing behavior. I was not given the tools to make good choices, because good choices are a result of healthy self-esteem. You basically have to re-program yourself, and how the heck does someone do that?

Every human being is conditioned by their experiences, and we all have a natural pull towards what is familiar, whether it is healthy or not, because the familiar feels safe. It is something that we at least know how to deal with. You spend 18 or so years figuring out how to get your needs met from someone who doesn't really care about your needs, so you know how to do that. It requires quite a lot of attention, patience, and self-sacrifice. Since you are skilled at this, when you encounter others who don't really care about anyone's needs but their own, you are just subconsciously attracted to them because it feels familiar. The people we love are usually giving us something we desire or think we need like love, support, relief, material help, inspiration, or ideas, so we latch on quickly and hold on tight. Then, like a leech, if the family member, lover, or friend is a narcissist, they begin to suck out all of our life-force.

If you have been raised in a culture that has already been doing this to the group of people you identify with, you are even more inclined to endure this kind of treatment and not even question it. This is especially true when the conditioning to endure the oppression has always included massive amounts of horrific violence. You are a part of a group that is simply terrified, justifiably, to reject their oppressors demands. It's why Black folk whisper, even when they are alone, about how much they can't stand some 'ofay' that is being shitty.

I really hope that it will become a new social dynamic that people are taught to pay attention to what they are attracted to. I hope that we will begin to ask questions like why do I like dark/light, tall/short, quiet/loud, small/large, feminine/masculine people? Questions that we also need to start asking are: What are truly healthy characteristics? What does courage really look like? How should you feel when someone loves you? How many roads are there to success? Does it absolutely REQUIRE a level of callousness? I mean, is there no other way to find comfort and security in the world outside of putting yourself before everyone else? There's got to be a more balanced way.

Since the narcissist who damaged you took so much from you, I also think on some level maybe, we feel like we can get it back if we find a way to work things out with someone who behaves a lot like them. So even after you have gotten away from the narcissist, you find yourself in the company of other dysfunctional people until you learn how to spot and avoid them. This comes after much suffering and loss. I don't know if it is absolutely inevitable, but I have never been aware of someone who was raised by a narcissist that grew up to make healthy relationship choices. So on top of all the physical and mental health problems that are more prevalent in abused and neglected children, you have to deal with the pain of constantly letting go of people and situations that are causing you harm. Since the mind and the soul seem to have a need to grow and evolve, which requires healing from trauma, we re-create traumatic circumstances until we heal. You simply cannot walk on a broken foot, and most of us want to fly!

Healing from trauma requires understanding, accepting, integrating, and then releasing an experience. One of the reasons we tell stories, write songs, and make movies about our experiences is to try to make sense of them. We have a need to recreate the stories of our lives in order to find a way to understand and heal from them. This is why we tend to find ourselves in similar experiences time and again once we become adults. We are trying to find a way out of the traumatic memories; trying to find a different ending; trying to reconcile with those who have hurt us. We interact with people that are similar to those who have hurt us to attempt a different outcome that will feel better. It's a huge part of developing self-esteem, and very much a part of the human experience; repetition is a key factor in learning as a child. You repeat something over and over, like tying your shoes, until you get it. You get into a relationship with abusive people over and over, until you find a way to escape and feel strong. It is of course almost impossible to see these patterns because attraction, lust, and love FEEL so intense and so real. It is hard to accept that we are conditioned to be attracted to certain kinds of people and situations. Since predators go after the most vulnerable, they are most attracted to abused people. It is the children who are not being looked after that are the most likely to be sexually abused, and thus become abusers themselves.

Richard Sipe from *Mea Maxima Culpa: Silence in the House of God* (2012) stated that the abuser "Plans activity, organizes situations to be able to abuse children ... Selects, cultivates, defends, and produces sexual abusers[5]." It is the children who are alone that get snatched off the street. This double whammy of having been abused or neglected when young, and then growing up to be abused and neglected by others is, to me, the most unfair part of having been raised by a narcissist. It is a life-long reconciliation.

I vividly remember Sinead O'Connor on *Saturday Night Live* ripping a picture of the Pope in half on live television. Everyone was horrified and her career was destroyed. Now we know she was telling the truth[6]. Now she suffers from mental illness.

I am still constantly facing my demons on a daily basis. There is not a year that goes by where I don't discover some other hidden aspect of myself that turns out to be something that has caused me a lot of pain over the years; some part of my personality that developed in adjustment to my crazy circumstances which initially served as a method of survival, but became a hindrance to my own well-being once I was out of the traumatic situation.

For instance, my mother would punish me anytime I spoke my mind, which was usually just stating something that I needed. Children need attention, food, regular sleep, help, etc... she just wasn't great at providing any of that, and she certainly didn't want it pointed out because that destroyed her image of herself as self-sacrificing and wonderful. Whatever I was really feeling or needing would get me into a lot of trouble. She would get furious when I was honest because it usually reflected something that she had done that was cruel. I quickly learned not to speak my mind, to keep quiet, and to stuff my feelings and needs deep down inside. Not so great for relationships! When you have not been taught how to fulfill your own needs, you are always dis-satisfied, and the person you are dealing with can feel that dis-satisfaction. Since nothing is being clarified, there are enough feelings of rejection, confusion, anger, and hurt to destroy any relationship. But it's so very hard to see that in the moment. It just feels like no one understands you, or that people don't care about you. It's so difficult to take challenges lightly, because most of the experiences you had while you were developing your personality that involved any kind of conflict ended in great harm being done to you. Or sometimes even total abandonment.

My mother often just left and did not take care of me, even when I was hurt or needed some kind of care, so I had to fend for myself. That is how I tend to approach my relationships—like I don't need anyone else. I just do everything myself, tell myself that I shouldn't expect anything from people, and the anger and resentment slowly builds when people aren't there for me. It is so incredibly difficult to go through life not trusting anyone. But it also makes you strong, independent, and skillful, so you appear to be a bad-ass, when really you are very damaged and in pain.

In addition, everyone wasn't raised by a narcissist, and most of us do not truly understand the nature of the condition. The majority of us have a few issues with our loved ones, but they do not generally prevent the relationship from continuing. I have found that most people find it very difficult to understand that you simply cannot have a relationship with a close relative like a mother or father because of how destructive the relationship is for you.

This is especially true as I have said, in oppressed communities like the African American community. We have had to be so united and have had to stick together to survive, so you are actually judged very harshly if you choose to separate from family. There is often little understanding for your trauma, and instead people see you as weak or judgmental. And let me tell you, the narcissist will also go out of their way to shape people's view of you, make themselves look good, and make you look crazy! I have lost many good people in my life who bought into the illusion that my mother projected in public, and who thus thought something must actually be wrong with me. Like most narcissists, my mother was quite well-known and popular.

Also, it is very important to understand that narcissists pick and choose who they will treat well and who they will treat poorly. They are not stupid; they are very strategic in their behavior. Father Murphy didn't molest hearing boys, he molested deaf boys—exclusively. Narcissists will not treat people who they depend on poorly. This was another trait of my mother's that helped me to open my eyes. It is another part of the narrative in how predators choose prey. They are very strategic in their choices and so was my mother. When I saw how kind she was to CERTAIN people, I knew that she had control over herself. That is when I was like "oh you are definitely not going to keep abusing me." People who I grew up with who did not know what was going on behind closed doors in our home, many of whom were even often a source of support for me, but who would never stop campaigning for my mother and for me to forgive her and to 'just let it go,' simply weren't aware what had been going on. They never saw her other side.

I have also found that it is difficult to maintain relationships due to health problems. Everyone just doesn't have a caretaker in them, and when you get sick a lot, which abused people often do, you find that you are on your own to deal with it. It is very difficult to not be hurt by that, and it tends to nurture a certain distance between you and others. I developed a belief that no one wanted to deal with my illnesses, and since they occurred quite often, I have wound up spending a lot of time alone. Before my daughter was born, I spent many holidays alone because I was sick or in pain, and I never seemed to be able to develop that circle of good friends I see so often depicted in movies.

It is so hard to fight off the constant feeling that something is wrong with you, that you will never be happy, and that you will be in pain until you die. It is challenging not to get emotional, even if you are internalizing it, about every little way that people may misunderstand you or express their own little dysfunctional wobbly parts because you are used to conflict and misunderstanding leading to freaking Armageddon for a day. You have absolutely no idea that you can tell someone they have hurt you, and that they might actually apologize and try to make it right because they care about you. It leads to very low expectations, and that does not lead to a happy life.

I asked myself agonizing questions most of my young life. It seemed everyone else was out having fun, while I was pondering: Why is life so hard for me? Why does it seem easier for others? Am I too sensitive? Am I stupid? Am I mentally ill? Am I cursed? Was I a horrible person in another lifetime? Why do I have such bad luck? Why can't I figure out how to just have a normal happy life? These are the questions I've been asking myself my entire life. It has felt to me like the world is a horrible, difficult place and I've spent much of my life simply trying to cope with the pain that I've been in enough to just make it to the end. I have often wished that the end would come sooner than later, and then suffered over the guilt of having those thoughts. The Christian dynamic that we live in has taught us that suicide is a sin, and that you will go to hell if you kill yourself, so the desire to just end it all causes even more guilt, and yet another toxic emotion for you to carry.

But there is also the curious reality of those times when you are not feeling so bad. There are times where everything seems to be going great! You are busy with life, love, and your personal goals. You are going to a job you hate, managing your relationships, and taking steps towards old and new dreams. We all watch the progress of others who seem to have figured out how to make things work. They are making money, doing things they enjoy, staying healthy (so it appears), and having relationships with friends, family, and those of the more intimate kind. We study the images of these people in the media and they are smiling and looking great and talking about how thankful they are. Many of them are giving to others and basically making a life that looks meaningful and exciting. I've always been fascinated by these people, paid attention to what they were doing, how they were doing it, and tried my best to apply these methodologies to my own life, and I managed to have extended periods of time when life seemed to make sense.

This time would inevitably collapse, usually as the result of a relationship ending, poor health, or economic stress. I would come to the conclusion that many of my problems were a result of my having dreams and goals that were not easy to achieve or in-line with what my family felt was appropriate. I got my degree in Theater and I always wanted to be a writer, a singer, an actress, and just live an artistic life in general. I didn't want to get a permanent job in a field that I didn't have a passion for, so I supported myself by doing temp-work in corporate and other business environments. It was so very difficult. Sitting in a chair behind a desk in an air-conditioned office seems to cause me very debilitating problems including back pain, neck pain, respiratory issues, fatigue, and eventually, depression. I am just not made for it.

Looking back now, it is fascinating to me how the root of my depression was something that just always lingered in the background of my life, like an unpleasant smell that you get used to after a while. There were always multiple sources of stress, pain, discomfort, confusion, and chaos that persisted through all of the normal life challenges, but there was always one presence that lingered behind every difficult circumstance like a ghost. But until I was well into my 30's, I was not able to identify this truth. Because I mean, I loved my mother! And she had a Ph.D. and was brilliant and funny and popular. It had to be me …

If anyone who is reading this feels this way, you are not alone. It takes a great amount of will-power and strength to deal with the life-long fall-out of narcissistic abuse, but there is hope! This narcissism epidemic is being publicized and discussed more and more, and there are increasingly accessible sources of support and information. I will list as many of them as I am aware of at the back of this book.

Please, don't give up! The world needs the wounded. We are the revealers of the hidden, and thus the true healers and civilizers of our world. We are going through a very difficult time in our history, and those of us who are able to recover and help others trying to recover are so valuable. Reach out to someone, don't stop trying, and try not to feel too bad about feeling hopeless sometimes. Many of us have good reason to feel that way, and it is only a sign that you are a feeling, loving, caring human being. There is no shame in sadness; no shame in hurt and pain. I truly believe that hurt and pain can be transformed into blindingly beautiful gifts. You are a gift. Let us see what is inside!

END

SUPERFICIAL SIGNS TO LOOK FOR

I want people to learn how to identify the signs of mental illness just as easily as we can identify signs of the common cold. There are behaviors that are quite common with bi-polar, depression, and border-line personality diagnoses. We just aren't taught this information at all. Here is a list of some things I think you should look out for to identify NPD:

1. acts like a toddler (sulks/throws tantrums/pouts/strikes out)
2. demanding/bossy
3. rude/inconsiderate (doesn't say please/thank you/excuse me)
4. tyrannical/temperamental (rage)
5. covert—always sick/overt—those around them sick
6. vacillates between highly intelligent and seemingly stupid
7. thinks they are smarter than everyone/thinks everyone is stupid
8. uses the word "I" a LOT
9. extremely materialistic/loves nice things
10. pathological liars/HYPER manipulative
11. always has a problem--every single day!
12. extremely paranoid—thinks everyone is 'out to get them'
13. HYPERsensitive--can't ever be wrong or at fault about ANYTHING. EVER.
14. extremely self-centered
15. will not change/may appear to change, but just pretending

This last one is so important! It's also where you lose a lot of people, because if there is one constant in life it is CHANGE. This is why to me, this particular element is crucial to understanding that this is a mental illness. These people don't follow the natural order of life. They may appear to change, but all they are really doing, is adjusting. They learn as they engage in conflict. They learn what to say and how to act to get people to capitulate, continue to engage with them, and for them to ultimately get their way. One of the smartest things I have heard from a psychiatrist is that the worst thing you can do is forgive a narcissist and take them back. It goes against everything we are taught about spirituality, but it is unfortunately good advice. If you forgive a narcissist for destroying your life, take them back and continue to engage with them, eventually, they will destroy you.

One of the ways narcissists destroy you, is with words. Verbal abuse is truly the worst. That old 'sticks and stones' saying is poppycock; words are so very powerful. Narcissists use words like weapons, and I have found that there are a few things they all seem to say.

Things they say:
"Look what you made me do!"
"How dare you!"
"We just had a misunderstanding"
"Don't take things so personal"
"You're hysterical calm down!"
"It is what it is"
"You're so dramatic/sensitive"
"You need a thicker skin"

In general, a narcissist will keep you arguing with them for hours. They LOVE to fight. They feed off of the energy of conflict. They keep you confused, going around in circles, and there will never be a solution. Alternatively, they will walk away and refuse to discuss anything. Covert narcissists will easily cry to get out of discussions. They will do and say anything to garner sympathy and get out of having to face themselves and make a change.

RESOURCES FOR INFORMATION AND SUPPORT

Documentaries/Series:
The Jinx (2015) HBO
Mea Maxima Culpa: Silence in the House of God (2012) HBO
Mommy Dead and Dearest (2017) HBO
Generation Wealth (2018) Amazon Prime
Crazywise (2017) Amazon Prime
Holy Hell (2016) Amazon Prime
Tiger King (2020) Netflix

There are so many books on narcissism that you can easily Google, so I wanted to give you a list of books that will actually help you heal from narcissistic abuse:

Books:
Gabor Mate's books: https://drgabormate.com/book/
Of Water and the Spirit (1994), Malidoma Patrice Some
Breaking the Habit of Being Yourself (2012), Dr. Joe Dispenza (really all of Dr. Joe's books!)
The Completion Process: The Practice of Putting Yourself Back Together Again (2016), Teal Swann

Websites:
Dr. Ramani Durvasula: https://www.youtube.com/c/DoctorRamani
Dr. Daniel Fox:
https://www.youtube.com/channel/UC932vfOwTbFni3GRrvVA6IQ
Dr. Gabor Mate: drgabormate.com
Malidoma Patrice Some: http://malidoma.com/main/
Dr. Joe Dispenza: https://drjoedispenza.com
Teal Swann: https://completionprocess.com
Meredith Miller: *Inner Integration*:
https://www.youtube.com/channel/UCrNg_13PdqKAZRPqyclRq1g

<u>List of movies/TV shows about narcissists:</u>

Brimstone (2016)
August: Osage County (2013)
The Sopranos (1999)
Joker (2019)
Mommie Dearest (1981)
The Last King of Scotland (2006)
The Apostle (1997)
One Flew Over the Cuckoo's Nest (1975)
Alexander (2004)
Caligula (1979)
White Oleander (2002)
American Psycho (2000)
Gone Girl (2014)
There Will Be Blood (2007)
Wall Street (1987)
Big Little Lies (2017)
Sharp Objects (2018) HBO
The Talented Mr. Ripley (1999)
The Wolf of Wall Street (2013)
Precious (2009)
The Dark Knight (2008)
Taxi Driver (1976)
Spotlight (2015)
Capone (2020) Netflix
Savage Grace (2007)
12 Years A Slave (2013)
Allen v. Farrow (2021) HBO

Pretty much every Mafia movie ever made!

ENDNOTES

Chapter 1

1. You can find this information on multiple websites including [https://www.cosmopolitan.com/entertainment/movies/g19738089/horror-movies-based-on-true-stories/] and [https://www.scoopwhoop.com/inothernews/horror-movies-based-on-true-stories/].
2. Watch: Real Stories. (2017, Oct. 2). *Inside Broadmoor/Real Stories* [Video]. YouTube. https://www.youtube.com/watch?v=-4BaCt5tlgI.
3. See: Bly, Nellie. *10 Days in a Mad-House.* New York, N.Y.: Ian L. Munro, 1877.
4. See: Cartwright, M. (2017, February 20). Narcissus. *Ancient History Encyclopedia.* Retrieved from https://www.ancient.eu/Narcissus/.
5. See: History.com editors. (2017, Sept. 13). *The Devil. A&E Television Networks.* Retrieved from: https://www.history.com/topics/folklore/history-of-the-devil.
6. From: (DSM, 2018) American Psychiatric Association. (2013). Diagnostic and statistical manual of mental disorders (5th ed.). Arlington, VA: Author.
7. (See above)
8. (See above)
9. See: CBS News. (n.d.). Celebrities With Chronic Health Conditions. Retrieved from: https://www.cbsnews.com/pictures/celebrities-with-chronic-health-conditions/9/.
10. See: Gorvett, Z. *The medications that change who we are.* BBC: Future/Psychology, Jan. 2020. Available at: https://www.bbc.com/future/article/20200108-the-medications-that-change-who-we-are.
11. Matto, Holly C. (Ed); Strolin-Goltzman, Jessica (Ed); Ballan, Michelle S. (Ed), (2014). Neuroscience for social work: Current research and

practice., (pp. 57-68). New York, NY, US: Springer Publishing Co, xxvi, 387 pp. It states:

Survivors of complex childhood trauma often struggle with their ability to experience compassion and empathy toward themselves and toward other people. Recent mindfulness literature has identified meditation as an evidence-supported intervention that is able to change the brain and increase one's capacity for experiencing empathy and compassion. This chapter offers an overview of selected literature on some of the effects of complex childhood trauma, and on mindfulness practices that can help to develop compassion and empathy toward one's self and toward others. A case study offers an illustration of the use of a meditative dialogue practice in psychotherapy with a survivor of complex childhood trauma that helped her develop her ability to experience empathy and compassion. (PsycINFO Database Record (c) 2015 APA, all rights reserved). Available at: https://www.researchgate.net/post/Is-there-a-correlation-between-trauma-and-empathy.

12. Ardiel, E. L., & Rankin, C. H. (2010). The importance of touch in development. *Paediatrics & child health*, *15*(3), 153–156. https://doi.org/10.1093/pch/15.3.153.
13. ABC News. (2018 Sept. 28). *Truth and Lies: Jonestown, Paradise Lost* [Video]. YouTube. https://www.youtube.com/watch?v=JUrd0h8-a6A.
14. Netflix. (2020 Feb. 26). *The Trials of Gabriel Fernandez* [Video]. YouTube. https://www.youtube.com/watch?v=-T7VXlB4qUI.
15. This is from part of Season 7, Episode 9 of *Deadly Women* that focused on Georgia Tann: (unknown writer/director). (Sept. 13, 2013). Above The Law. [Television series episode]. (Beyond International), Deadly Women. Investigation Discovery.
16. (See above)
17. (See above)

Chapter 2

1. Sigmund Freud was known for his psychosexual theory and Erik Erikson for his psychosocial theory on childhood development. An article that generally sums them up is: Cherry, K. (2019 Oct. 29). Comparing Erikson's vs. Freud's Theories. *very well mind.* https://www.verywellmind.com/freud-and-erikson-compared-2795959.

2. Burke Harris, N. (2014, September). *Nadine Burke Harris: How childhood trauma affects health across a lifetime* [Video file]. Nadine Burke Harris. Retrieved from: https://www.ted.com/talks/nadine_burke_harris_how_childhood_trauma_affects_health_across_a_lifetime?language=en.

3. Aratani, L. 'Tsunami of untruths': Trump has made 20,000 false or misleading claims – report. The Guardian. July 13, 2020. Available at: https://www.theguardian.com/us-news/2020/jul/13/donald-trump-20000-false-or-misleading-claims.

4. See: Goldfarb, K. (2018, March 16). Barbara Daly Baekeland Tried To Cure Her Son's Homosexuality With Incest — Instead He Killed Her. Allthatsinteresting.com. Retrieved from: https://allthatsinteresting.com/barbara-daly-baekeland. Also see the movie *Savage Grace* (2007): https://www.amazon.com/Savage-Grace-Julianne-Moore/dp/B001NDYILA/ref=as_li_ss_tl?s=movies-tv&ie=UTF8&qid=1526071228&sr=1-1&keywords=savage+grace&linkCode=ll1&tag=probefhos-20&linkId=505037d0770a3b2b6358f2322629e1c8.

5. There is so much evidence of this, it is hard to pick just one. This is a good place to start: https://allthatsinteresting.com/pederasty.

6. See: Skinner, B. F. (1938). *The Behavior of Organisms*. pp. 117. N.Y.: D. Appleton-Century Co.

7. (See above)

Chapter 3

1. See: Trump, M.L. (2020). Too Much and Never Enough: How my family created the world's most dangerous man. Simon & Schuster.

2. See: MacKenzie, C. (1992). Psychiatry for the Rich: A History of Ticehurst Private Asylum. 1st ed. London, UK. Routledge. doi: https://doi.org/10.4324/9780203984017.

3. See: Shorter, E. (1997). A history of psychiatry: From the era of the asylum to the age of Prozac. John Wiley & Sons.

ENDNOTES

4. This is depicted in the Biographical movie *The Madness of King George* (1994) and can be found in many references including: Butterfield, Herbert. (1965). Some Reflections on the Early Years of George III's Reign. *Journal of British Studies.* **4** (2): 78–101. doi:10.1086/385501.

5. From: Slavevoyages.org at: https://slavevoyages.org/assessment/estimates.

6. From: Porter, R. (2006). *Madmen: A social history of madhouses, Mad-Doctors, & Lunatics.* Tempus.

7. (See above)

8. From: CBS This Morning. (2019 Dec. 14). Living in a Former Asylum. *CBS Interactive Inc.* Available at: https://www.cbsnews.com/news/traverse-city-state-hospital-former-asylum-in-michigan-transformed-into-new-apartments/.

9. See at: statista.com. (2020, August). Number of mental health facilities in the U.S. in 2019, by facility type. https://www.statista.com/statistics/712614/mental-health-facilities-number-in-the-us-by-facility-type/.

10. See: Fakhoury W, Priebe S. (2007). *Deinstitutionalization and Reinstitutionalization: Major changes in the provision of mental healthcare.* Psychiatry; 6:313–16.

11. Found on the CDC website here: https://www.cdc.gov/nchs/products/databriefs/db377.htm,

12. Found in the Netflix documentary *Take Your Pills:* Hepburn, C., Goldman, J., Clements, C. (Producers), & Klayman, A. (Director). 2018. *Take Your Pills* [Video file]. Retrieved from: https://www.netflix.com/title/80117831.

13. Find in: Matsumoto, D., & Juang, L. (2008). *Culture and psychology* (4th ed.). Belmont, CA: Thomson Wadsworth.

14. See: History.com. *Slavery in America.* A&E Television Networks, LLC. 11/12/2009. Available at: https://www.history.com/topics/black-history/slavery.

15. See: Bergeron, D. M. (1999). *King James and Letters of Homoerotic Desire.* Iowa City: University of Iowa Press, p. 348.

16. See: Ardiel, E. L., & Rankin, C. H. (2010). The importance of touch in development. Paediatrics & child health, 15(3), 153–156. https://doi.org/10.1093/pch/15.3.153.
17. See: Burke Harris, N. (2014, September). *Nadine Burke Harris: How childhood trauma affects health across a lifetime* [Video file]. Nadine Burke Harris. Retrieved from: https://www.ted.com/talks/nadine_burke_harris_how_childhood_traum a_affects_health_across_a_lifetime?language=en.

Chapter 4

1. ABC News. (2018 Sept. 28). Truth and Lies: Jonestown, Paradise Lost [Video]. YouTube. https://www.youtube.com/watch?v=JUrd0h8-a6A. A survivor stated: "People think they willingly died," she says, "but Jones gave them no choice. They were surrounded by a row of guards with crossbows, and then behind them there was another line of guards pointing guns. Meanwhile, Jones is exhorting them to come up and drink this potion to take them to the other side. So, living was never an alternative on that last night. Most people chose to die with their families, and if they didn't drink it, there were many who were injected with the poison."
2. (See above)
3. See: Irving, K., Christensen, D. (Producers), & Wolochatiuk, T. (Director). (2012). *We Were Children*. [Video file]. Retrieved from: https://www.nfb.ca/film/we_were_children/trailer/we_were_children_t railer/. See also this article on another documentary: Millich, G. (2020). Survivors of Indian Boarding Schools tell their stories. *WKAR News, Michigan State University*. https://www.wkar.org/post/survivors-indian-boarding-schools-tell-their-stories#stream/0.
4. See: Dutton, K. (2012). The Wisdom of Psychopaths: What Saints, Spies, and Serial Killers Can Teach Us About Success. *Scientific American*.
5. See: Sorvino, C. (2016, March 5). Aubrey McClendon's Sad Death And 8 Other Tragic Stories Involving The Super Rich. *Forbes.com magazine*. Find at: https://www.forbes.com/sites/chloesorvino/2016/03/05/aubrey-mcclendons-sad-death-and-eight-other-tragic-stories-involving-the-super-rich/#7746b3816b55.

6. Find at: Cate. (2018, June 21). Famous Heirs/Heiress: The Forgotten Tragedies. *Fame10.com magazine.* https://www.fame10.com/entertainment/famous-heirsheiress-12-forgotten-tragedies/.

7. (See above)

Chapter 5

1. See the Iroquois constitution here: Murphy, G. (1997, August). Modern History Sourcebook: The Constitution of the Iroquois Confederacy. Fordham University. Retrieved from: https://sourcebooks.fordham.edu/mod/iroquois.asp.

2. See: Durvasula R. (n.d.). *DoctorRamani* [YouTube channel]. Retrieved from: https://www.youtube.com/c/DoctorRamani and, Fox, D. (n.d.). Dr. Daniel Fox [YouTube channel]. Retrieved from: https://www.youtube.com/channel/UC932vfOwTbFni3GRrvVA6IQ.

3. Yochelson, S., & Samenow, S.E. (1976). The Criminal Personality: A Profile for Change. New York: J. Aronson. Available at: https://www.worldcat.org/title/criminal-personality/oclc/645790089.

Chapter 6

1. From the Netflix Documentary *Trump: An American Dream*. Glover, D., Raphael, M. (Producers) & Peel, B., Bogado, D., Zinni, N. (Directors). (2017). [Video file]. Retrieved from: https://www.netflix.com/title/80206395.

2. See: Devaney, J. (2020, Oct. 1). My Thoughts on "Spiritual Narcissism." *Collective-Evolution.com.* Find at: https://www.collective-evolution.com/2020/10/19/my-thoughts-on-spiritual-narcissism/?vgo_ee=JWkFMc0P%2F2gOYhYAkKAz9DpxdzkQNl9LgdxZ9pnzLRY%3D)/.

3. See: Greenfield, L., Evers, F., Annenberg, W. (Producers), & Greenfield, L. (Director). (2018). Generation Wealth. Evergreen Pictures.

4. The Sackler Family owns Purdue Pharma (who produced OxyContin) and they have plead guilty to federal felony charges of misleading consumers on the risks of addiction and abuse for OxyContin, which is the main culprit in the U.S. opioid epidemic. The family, whose wealth reaches the world of art, fashion, and education, according to this article in The Guardian is now feuding: Walters, J. (2018, Feb. 13). Meet the Sacklers: the family feuding over blame for the opioid crisis. TheGuardian.com. https://www.theguardian.com/us-news/2018/feb/13/meet-the-sacklers-the-family-feuding-over-blame-for-the-opioid-crisis

5. See: Gibney, A., Wider, T., Wider, J., Vaurio, K. (Producers), Gibney, A. (Director). 2012. Mea Maxima Culpa: Silence in the House of God. HBO. Jigsaw Productions.

6. See Sinead O'Connor ripping pic of pope in half on SNL: Dr. Phil. (2017). Why Sinead O'Connor Says She Ripped Up A Picture Of The Pope On Live TV [video]. Retrieved from: YouTube.https://www.youtube.com/watch?v=pkumnOW1xRk.